Abstract

When I was fresher, I can't understand the concept, there is no proper material to learn myself. Now I am good in concept also created this file which contains the entire AR CALLER/Medical billing concept in one shop. Even fresher can understand on their own without any trainer's help. Let's open it and understand the concept by yourself!.

Follow us in YouTube V BILLINGS

Vijayakumar Munusamy

V Billings

AR Training, AR Refreshing, JOB assistance & placement for both fresher and experienced

Contact V BILLINGS

Email: vijaisun11@gmail.com

FOLLOW US/Join in VBILLINGS FAMILY:

Website: https://vbcareer.com/

YouTube:
https://www.youtube.com/channel/UCtqFFg9hxpUn8xHarCqcgeg

Instagram: https://www.instagram.com/vbcareer/

LinkedIn: https://www.linkedin.com/in/vbcareer-vbillings-52838b209/

Facebook: https://www.facebook.com/Vbcareer-100379945475868

Telegram: https://t.me/vbillings

Email: vijaisun11@gmail.com

Subscribe to our YouTube Channel: V BILLINGS

What is MEDICAL BILLING?

Medical billing is the process for creating and submitting claims to the insurance company to receive payment for the treatment provided by the doctor to patients.

Future of medical billing professions in India:

Medical Billing, Medical Coding, AR calling, and AR analyst having a bright future in India. USA Healthcare Market increase day by day with more complicated Disease and more big Hospital and Medical Organization. Currently, India is a hub for data Processing and data solution services. Right now, India gets outsourcing from the USA and there are many possibilities the UK, Australia, and Canada also will join the list shortly.

Why India remains at the top in the outsourcing hub? there are many reasons particularly significant cost savings that companies can achieve. Also India has young, educated & energetic associates who provide consistently high-quality services.

AR caller, you will be responsible for making calls to insurance companies to follow up on pending claims

What is RCM (Revenue Cycle Management)?

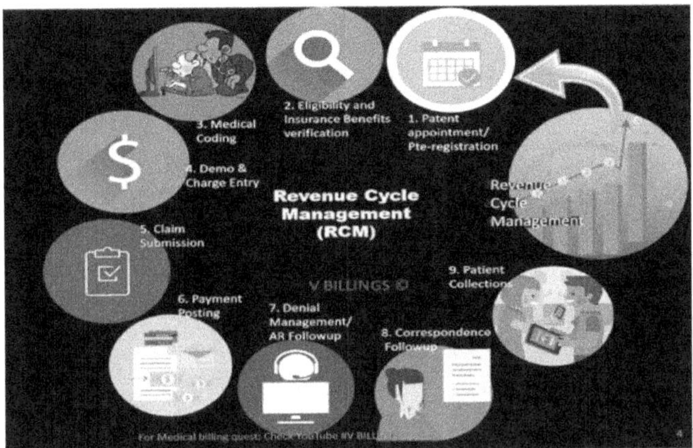

Healthcare revenue cycle management begins when the patient makes the appointment to seek medical services and ends with successful payment collection.

1.Patent appointment/Preregistration

2.Eligibility and Insurance Benefits verification:

3. Medical Coding

4.Demo & Charge Entry

5.Claim Submission

6.Payment Posting

7.Denial Management/AR Follow-up

8.Correspondence Follow-up

9.Patient Collections

1.Patent appointment/Preregistration:

Revenue Cycle Management (RCM) starts with the patient's appointment. A patient can get a doctor's appointment by call, online, or by visiting the doctor's office/hospital. An appointment should at least 48 hours prior. Once the Appointment is scheduled, necessary information like patient demographics, insurance details, and reason for visit, etc are taken.

2.Eligibility and Insurance Benefits verification:

After the patient's appointment, patient eligibility and benefits are checked with patient insurance to verify that the services that the patient will get are covered or not by insurance. Other details like Co-pay, Coinsurance, Deductible, Prior authorization are obtained during this process. Once eligibility and benefits verification was completed, the patient will get the treatment from the doctor at the scheduled time.

The treatment given to the patient is recorded on the superbill, EMR, or in the form of voice (Dicta Phone), etc.

3.Medical Coding

Medical coders review the complete medical records and convert them into codes. On the claim form patient Diagnosis (ICD), Current Procedural Terminology (CPT), and Healthcare Common Procedure Coding System (HCPCS) are used.

4. Demo & Charge Entry:

Once all the essential information is gathered, it's time to enter those data on the claim form or in the billing software. Here the claim form will be created with all the billing details, service details, provider details, patient details, and insurance details. A claim form can be filled in by hand or via using the billing software.

5.Claim Submission:

After the charge entry, it's time to send the claim form to the insurance company to get paid for the services rendered by the Healthcare providers

3 types of claim submissions:

1.Paper claim

2.Electronic claim submission (clearing house)

3.Online claim entry on an insurance web portal.

6.Payment Posting:

When the claim gets approved for payment, the insurance company sends paid EOB or ERA along with payment. The EOB is posted manually or electronically by the payment posting team.

Payment will be issued through different modes of transmissions:

1.Paper Check

2.EFT (Electronic Fund Transfer)

3.Virtual Credit card

7.Denial Management/AR Follow-up:

This process includes Insurance follow-ups, claims status checks, resolution of denied/rejected claims, preparing appeal letters, etc.

8.Correspondence Follow-up:

After the EOB has been received from the payer, now biller will make the statement for the patient.

After the payer has paid the provider for a portion of the services on the claim as per contract, the remaining portion is passed to the patient. A biller may include an EOB with the statement. EOBs can be useful in explaining to the patient why certain services were covered while others were not.

9.Patient Collections:

It is the process of collecting the payment from the patient when there is reduced reimbursement from the payers, it means the health plan does not cover all the services.

This is the duty of the billers to send those outstanding payments to the patient by generating a Patient statement and follow-up.

Follow-up may involve contacting the patient directly, sending follow-up bills.

In worst-case scenarios, at last, collection agency follow-ups until the patients finally pay up.

AR TEAM:

AR Analyst (Day Shift)

AR follow-up / AR Caller (Night Shift)

AR Analyst (Day Shift):

The AR Analysis team is responsible for reviewing and analyzing pended claims as well as partial payments. If any claim is found to have a coding error, the AR team corrects it and resubmits the claim.

AR Caller / AR follow-up (Night Shift):

The AR Caller team on the other hand constantly communicates with healthcare providers, patients, and insurance companies through phone calls and takes necessary actions based on their feedback or responses.

The skills and quality of services delivered by the AR team eventually help in determining the financial health of a healthcare provider.

Calling team:

The call-center setup where the employees from the company will contact USA healthcare insurance companies in order to get the claim status over the phone call.

Calling can be generally classified into three types.

1) Doctor calling

2) Insurance Calling and

3) 3) Patient Calling

1) Doctor Calling:

Calling the Doctor's office by the caller for any patient's information, procedure information, etc.

2) Insurance Calling:

Another name is AR CALLER, here the caller calls the insurance company, gets the information on what happened on that claim and conveys it to the AR Analyst to act on it.

3) Patient Calling:

The caller calls up the patient for various reasons. When there is no response from the patient. Insurance information, Insurance coverage, Patient statement, Documents needed from a patient in order to move the pended claim to the next processing stage.

Accounts Receivables department - the backbone of Medical Billing.

3 Ps in medical billing:

1.PATIENT

2.PROVIDER

3.PAYER

1. Who is the Patient (Insurer/subscriber/dependent/policyholder)?

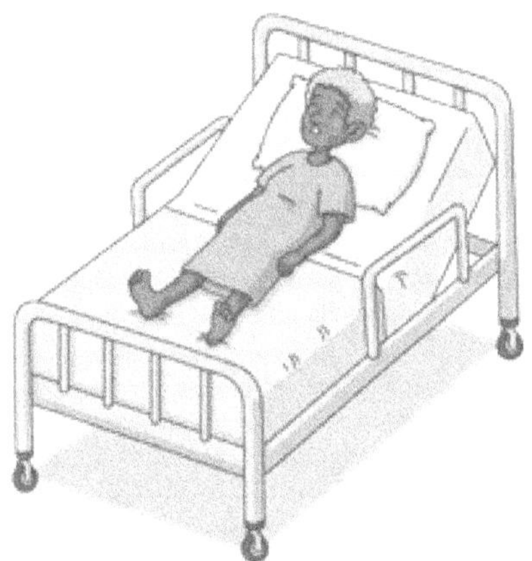

The person who gets medical services from the provider. Other names Insurer/subscriber/dependent/policyholder.

2. Who is the Provider (Doctors, physicians, surgeons, technicians, hospitals, clinics, laboratories)?

The individual or an organization who provides medical services to the patient

3. Who is Payer (Insurance company)?

The individual or an organization that processes the claim and pays the provider for the medical services are given to the patient.

DEMO entry (Patient's Demographic)?

It is the process of entering the patient details into the provider software.

Demographic details to be entered are as follows:

1.Patient's details (Account #, Name, age, sex,address,SSN,marital status,telephone #, etc,.)

2.Patient's Insurance details

3.COB (Coordination of benefits)

4.ROI (Release of information)

5.AOB (Assignment of benefits)

6.ABN (Advanced Beneficiary Notice)/WOL (Wavier of liability)

7.Patient's guarantor details

8.Patient's Employer details

1.Patient Name:

Entered as Last name, First Name, Middle Initial.

Example:

Linda K Janes can be written as Janes, Linda K

2. Patient Date of Birth:

Entered in the format MM/DD/YYYY or MMDDYYYY.

3. Patient SSN:

It contains a 9 digits number which is allotted to the patient by the Social Security Administration

4.Patient phone number:

It contains the contact number of the patient including the area code. It contains a total of 10 digits (111-222-3333), the first 3 digits are the area code, and the next 7 digits are the phone number of the patient.

Encounter process?

It is the conversation between provider and patient.

Here the patient will explain to the doctor about the illness facing and the doctor will give medication to the patient.

During this process, the conversation including diagnosis (DX) and Procedure (CPT) is recorded in Dictaphone as a voice file

Transcription process?

It is the process of converting the voice file into a text file.

The transcript text sheets are called Transcribed sheets.

Medical Coding process?

It is the process of assigning numeric and alphanumeric codes to the service/treatment (diagnosis and procedure). In this process CPT code, diagnosis code, and modifier were entered.

Charge sheets/Super Bills:

Name of Clinic
Address Line 1
Address Line 2

SUPERBILL TEMPLATE

Date of Service:	Insurance Provider:
Patient ID:	Insurance ID:
Patient Name:	Provider:
Patient Date of Birth:	
Patient Gender (circle one): M / F	

Evaluation and Management Codes (Time in Minutes)		Codes	CPT	$	Laboratory Codes		Codes	CPT	$
New Patient Office Visit	Problem Focused-Straightforward (10 min)		99201		UHCG-Urine Pregnancy			81025	
	Expanded Problem Focused-Straightforward (20 min)		99202		Wet mount			87210	
	Detailed-Low Complexity (30 min)		99203		Venipuncture			36415	
	Comprehensive-Moderate Complexity (45 min)		99204		PPD Plant TB			86580	
Established patient visit	Follow-up (presenting problems minimal) (5 min)		99211		Gram Stain			87205	
	Problem Focused-Straightforward (10 min)		99212		Urinalysis (Dip stick)			81003	
	Expanded Problem Focused-Low Complexity (15 min)		99213		Glucose-Fingerstick			82962	
	Detailed-Moderate Complexity (25 min)		99214		Total Cholesterol Screening (HDL, LDL +TRG)			80061	
	Detailed - High Complexity (40 min)		99215		Rapid HIV-1/Initial CMS test			86701	
Procedure Codes					Rapid HIV-1/2			86703	
Injection Administration-Medication	Subcutaneous or Intramuscular		96372		Hep C-Rapid			87902	
Other Procedures					STD Tests	Labs sent to State Lab for Processing-Use for Tracking Only			
Wart Removal (Simple vs Extensive- Provide)	Vulva; simple		56501						
	Vulva; extensive		56515		VDRL - Syphilis				

It is a kind of sheet that consists of the list of services provided by a particular provider, it also includes other information like appointment/visit information, CPT and ICD codes, patient information, and provider information.

It is important to note that the superbill should only outline the medical services mentioned in the patient's insurance plan because the insurance company will not pay for the services that fall outside the insurance plan.

Super Bills, also called Charge Slips, Fee Tickets, or Encounter forms.

Charge Entry process?

The charge entry process is where your claims are created.

Charge entry is the process of assigning appropriate $(Dollar) value to the patient account.

Once the patient information and service information has been received from the client as a scanned copy of the superbill/charge ticket, these files are downloaded from the FTP site then the following charge entry process will happen.

.

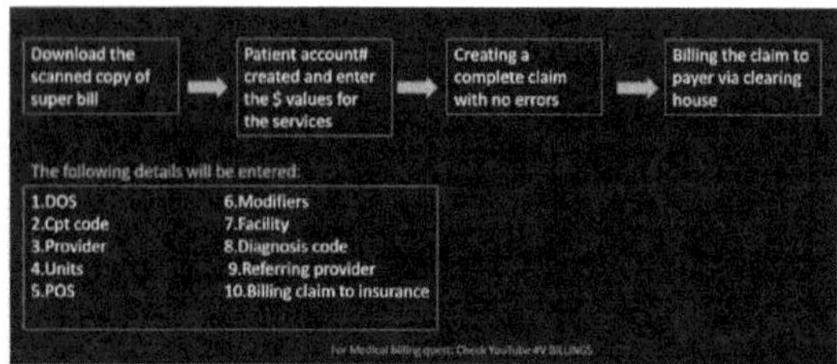

Diagnosis code (illness/sickness)?

Diagnosis code (Dx code) is a combination of letters and/or numbers assigned to particular illness/sickness, symptoms, or procedure.

Diagnosis code is developed by WHO as (ICD code) International Classification of Disease.

ICD code is redesigned by (CMS) Centers for Medicare & Medicaid Services

CMS revises this regularly:

ICD-9-CM (9th Revision Clinical Mod

ICD-10-CM (10th Revision Clinical Modification)

Example:

E08.3293 denotes Diabetes mellitus due to underlying condition with mild nonproliferative diabetic retinopathy without macular edema, bilateral

CMS Box 21 Up to 12 diagnoses can be reported in the header on the Form CMS-1500 paper claim and, up to 8 diagnoses can be reported in the header on the electronic claim.

Diagnosis code volume I:

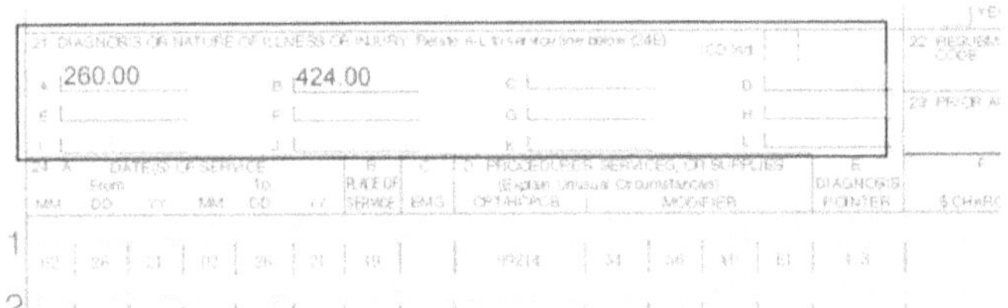

These Dx codes are used to find the illness/symptoms and diseases of the patient

Example: E08.3293 denotes Diabetes mellitus due to underlying condition with mild nonproliferative diabetic retinopathy without macular edema, bilateral

Format: xxx. xxx.x. Xxx.xx

Diagnosis code volume II:

E- Code:

These codes represent the External cause of injury

Example: E881.0, Fall from a ladder

Format: Exxx. Exxx.x

V- Code:

These codes used for visits to a health care professional for purposes other than for sickness/disease/illness/injury (e.g., physicals, immunizations, pregnancies, Donar of an organ etc,..).
Example: V70.0 Routine general medical examination at a healthcare facility
Format: Vxx. Vxx.x. Vxx.xx

Diagnosis pointer (Box# 24E)?

24 A. DATE(S) OF SERVICE From MM	DD	YY	To MM	DD	YY	B PLACE OF SERVICE	C EMG	D. PROCEDURES, SERVICES, OR SUPPLIES (Explain Unusual Circumstances) CPT/HCPCS	MODIFIER			E DIAGNOSIS POINTER	F $ CHARGES
1	02	26	21	02	26	21	19		99214	54	56	XU	1 3	
2	02	26	21	02	26	21	19		1090F	LT	XE		1	
3	02	26	21	02	26	21	19		4090F	RT	XS		2	
4	02	26	21	02	26	21	19		3048F				1	
5														
6														

A pointer to the claim diagnosis code in the order of importance to this service. Use this pointer for the first diagnosis code pointer (primary diagnosis for this service line).

Enter the diagnosis code reference letter as shown in Item 21 to relate the date of service and the procedures performed to the primary diagnosis. Enter only one reference letter per line item. When multiple services are performed, enter the primary reference letter for each service. This will be a letter from A to L.

Although you can list up to 12 diagnosis codes on a claim, the number of diagnosis code pointers for each service line in box 24E is limited to four per line. Please label the 10th, 11th, and 12th diagnosis codes and their corresponding diagnosis code pointers with the letters J, K, and L.

CPT CODE:

CPT - Current Procedural Terminology

Designed by - American Medical Association (AMA)

Year - 1966

CPT - 5 Digits Numeric, Alpha, Alpha Numeric

Why the CPT code created?
To standardized reporting of medical, surgical, and diagnostic services and procedures performed in in-patient and out-patient settings

Example:
99214 used for an office visit,
90716 used for chickenpox vaccine(varicella).

CPT CODE Facts:
Will all the doctors get the same payment for CPT CODE?
Ans: No, Reimbursed will not necessarily be the same

For example, Doctor "A" may perform a physical check-up (99396) and he reimbursed $100 from insurance.

The same checkup performed by another Doctor "B" he reimbursed for $90 from insurance. This is determined by the contracts between a particular provider and the insurance company.

Category of CPT codes:

Category I - The existing codes consisting of those commonly used by providers to report their services and procedures

Category II - Supplemental tracking code used for performance measurements

Category III - Temporary codes used to report emerging and experimental services and procedures

Category I CPT CODE:

The existing codes consisting of those commonly used by providers to report their services and procedures

Approved by Food and Drug Administration (FDA)

Format- Five digits Numeric

6 Sections of Category I CPT code:

1) Evaluation and Management: 99201 - 99499

2) Anesthesia: 00100 - 01999; 99100 - 99140

3) Surgery   10021 - 69990

4) Radiology: 70010 - 79999

5) Pathology and Laboratory: 80047 - 89398

6) Medicine: 90281 - 99199; 99500 - 99607

Category II CPT CODE:

Supplemental tracking code used for performance measurements

A provider can assign in addition to Category I code

Category I codes are not linked to reimbursement

Format- Four numbers and the letter F

Examples:
1.If a doctor records a patient's Body Mass Index (BMI) during a routine checkup, we could use Category II code 3008F, here Body Mass Index (BMI) documented

2.Doctors use this code to track specific information about their patients, such as whether they use tobacco to help them deliver better healthcare and achieve better outcomes for their patients.

Examples:
Composite Measures 0001F-0015F
Patient Management 0500F-0575F
Patient History 1000F-1220F
Physical Examination 2000F-2050F

Category III CPT CODE:

Temporary codes that represent new technology, service, and procedure.

Format- Four numbers and the letter T

The AMA(American Medical Association) releases new or revised category III codes semi-annually via their website but publishes the Category III deletions annually with the full set of temporary codes.

Temporary codes describing new services and the procedure can remain in Category III for up to five years. If the services and procedures they represent meet Category I criteria which includes FDA approval, evidence that many providers perform the procedures, and evidence that the procedures have proven effective-they will be reassigned Category I codes. Conversely, Category III codes can be eliminated if providers do not use them.

LEVELS OF CPT CODES:

Level I (DOCTOR) codes consist of the AMA's CPT code.
Format: 5 Digits Numeric.

Level II (HOSPITAL) codes are HCPCS (Health Common Procedure Coding System) it includes non-physician products, supplies, and procedures not included in CPT.
Format: 5 Digits Alpha-Numeric.

Level III codes, also HCPCS local codes, were developed by state Medicaid agencies, Medicare contractors, and private insurers for use in specific programs and jurisdictions. These codes are still included in the HCPCS reference coding book. Some payers that coders report that Level III codes in addition to the Level I and

Level II code sets. However, these codes are not nationally recognized

Format: Start with an alphabet X or Z followed by Four Digits Numeric like HCPCS level II codes.

Modifiers:

24. A DATE(S) OF SERVICE From			To			B PLACE OF SERVICE	C EMG	D. PROCEDURES, SERVICES, OR SUPPLIES (Explain Unusual Circumstances) CPT/HCPCS	MODIFIER				E DIAGNOSIS POINTER	$ CH.
MM	DD	YY	MM	DD	YY									
02	26	21	02	26	21	19		99214	54	56	XU	EJ	1 3	
02	26	21	02	26	21	19		10908	LT	XE			1	
02	26	21	02	26	21	19		3085F	RT	XS			2	
02	26	21	02	26	21	19		3648F					1	

Modifiers are added to CPT or HCPCS codes it gives additional information to the service without changing the service's original meaning

They are added to the end of a CPT/HCPCS codes with a hyphen (e.g   19302-LT)

Most modifiers are numeric though a few are alphanumeric

Format: Two digits Alpha/Numeric/Alpha Numeric

Example: LT- -Procedure on the left side of the body, 50- Bilateral procedure

Claim filing methods:

The most common methods are two:

Electronic (Claim sent through clearing house)

Paper(Claim sent through post or mail)

Electronic claim submission:

Electronic claims or E claims are submitted through clearinghouses. The clearinghouse will check the claims for errors if an error is found then the claim will never send to insurance, it will get rejected which is called clearinghouse rejections. Once the errors have been rectified manually then the claim will resubmit, again the clearinghouse will check for errors if no error is found then the claim will send to insurance by converting the claim's format to the insurance-specific format which is called a clean claim.

After the payer received the claim payer end will check for an error that has been missed from the clearinghouse, if the payer end found an error again the claim will get rejected which is called payer end rejections.

Examples of Clearinghouses: Availity, Navient, Gateway, etc,.

Scrubber report:

The clearinghouse will generate the Scrubber report this report contains a number of claims that were received to the clearinghouse, how many passed to the insurance company, and how many not passed to the insurance company.

What is the purpose of claim scrubbers?

The claim scrubber verifies CPT/HCPCS Level II codes and ICD-10-CM codes. The scrubber looks at the procedure code and diagnosis code to justify the medical necessity of the procedure.

Paper claim submission:

Claim sent through post or mail.
Submission of the CMS 1500 claim form should either be typed or computer-printed forms. Handwritten forms can cause delays and errors in processing and slow down time for reimbursement.

Claim forms two types:

1.HCFA/CMS 1500 (Doctor/Professional claim form):

1500

HEALTH INSURANCE CLAIM FORM

APPROVED BY NATIONAL UNIFORM CLAIM COMMITTEE 08/05

PICA

Humana
PO Box 14610
Lexington KY 40512-4610

CARRIER

1. MEDICARE MEDICAID TRICARE CHAMPUS CHAMPVA GROUP HEALTH PLAN FECA BLK LUNG OTHER

1a. INSURED'S I.D. NUMBER (For Program in Item 1)
890456732

2. PATIENT'S NAME (Last Name, First Name, Middle Initial)
DOE, John

3. PATIENT'S BIRTH DATE   SEX
06 15 1955   M [X] F

4. INSURED'S NAME (Last Name, First Name, Middle Initial)
DOE, John

5. PATIENT'S ADDRESS (No., Street)
1234 Main Street

6. PATIENT RELATIONSHIP TO INSURED
Self [X] Spouse Child Other

7. INSURED'S ADDRESS (No., Street)
1234 Main Street

CITY Anywhere STATE CA

8. PATIENT STATUS
Single Married Other [X]

CITY Anywhere STATE CA

ZIP CODE 90210 TELEPHONE (Include Area Code) (987)654-3210

Employed [X] Full Time Student Part Time Student

ZIP CODE 90210 TELEPHONE (Include Area Code) (987)654-3210

9. OTHER INSURED'S NAME (Last Name, First Name, Middle Initial)

10. IS PATIENT'S CONDITION RELATED TO:

11. INSURED'S POLICY GROUP OR FECA NUMBER
AN905-678

a. OTHER INSURED'S POLICY OR GROUP NUMBER

a. EMPLOYMENT? (Current or Previous)
YES [X] NO

a. INSURED'S DATE OF BIRTH   SEX
06 15 1955   M [X] F

b. OTHER INSURED'S DATE OF BIRTH   SEX

b. AUTO ACCIDENT? PLACE (State)
YES [X] NO

b. EMPLOYER'S NAME OR SCHOOL NAME
Universal Studios

c. EMPLOYER'S NAME OR SCHOOL NAME

c. OTHER ACCIDENT?
YES [X] NO

c. INSURANCE PLAN NAME OR PROGRAM NAME
Humana

d. INSURANCE PLAN NAME OR PROGRAM NAME

10d. RESERVED FOR LOCAL USE

d. IS THERE ANOTHER HEALTH BENEFIT PLAN?
YES NO If yes, return to and complete item 9 a-d.

READ BACK OF FORM BEFORE COMPLETING & SIGNING THIS FORM.

12. PATIENT'S OR AUTHORIZED PERSON'S SIGNATURE
SIGNED Signature On File   DATE 01 21 2011

13. INSURED'S OR AUTHORIZED PERSON'S SIGNATURE
SIGNED Signature On File

14. DATE OF CURRENT ILLNESS, INJURY OR PREGNANCY (LMP)

15. IF PATIENT HAS HAD SAME OR SIMILAR ILLNESS. GIVE FIRST DATE

16. DATES PATIENT UNABLE TO WORK IN CURRENT OCCUPATION
FROM TO

17. NAME OF REFERRING PROVIDER OR OTHER SOURCE
17b. NPI

18. HOSPITALIZATION DATES RELATED TO CURRENT SERVICES
FROM TO

19. RESERVED FOR LOCAL USE
Op rpt attached

20. OUTSIDE LAB?
[X] YES NO $ CHARGES 250 00   0 00

21. DIAGNOSIS OR NATURE OF ILLNESS OR INJURY
1. 525 25
2. 785 6

22. MEDICAID RESUBMISSION CODE   ORIGINAL REF. NO

23. PRIOR AUTHORIZATION NUMBER
567890456

24. A. DATE(S) OF SERVICE From / To MM DD YY MM DD YY	B. PLACE OF SERVICE	C. EMG	D. PROCEDURES, SERVICES, OR SUPPLIES CPT/HCPCS	MODIFIER	E. DIAGNOSIS POINTER	F. $ CHARGES	G. DAYS OR UNITS	H. EPSDT Family Plan	I. ID. QUAL	J. RENDERING PROVIDER ID #
JO01 02 21 11 02 21 11	11		21248		1	6000 00	3		NPI	8934267812
02 21 11 02 21 11	11		21210	99 51 52	1	3000 00	1		NPI	8934267812
ZZ Interim prosthesis JO01 02 21 11 02 21 11	11		21089		1	1200 00	1		NPI	8934267812
									NPI	
									NPI	
									NPI	

25. FEDERAL TAX I.D. NUMBER SSN EIN [X]
364246789

26. PATIENT'S ACCOUNT NO.
1234

27. ACCEPT ASSIGNMENT?
YES [X] NO

28. TOTAL CHARGE $ 10200 00
29. AMOUNT PAID $ 0 00
30. BALANCE DUE $ 10200 00

31. SIGNATURE OF PHYSICIAN OR SUPPLIER INCLUDING DEGREES OR CREDENTIALS
Olya Zahrebelny DDS
SIGNED   02 21 2011 DATE

32. SERVICE FACILITY LOCATION INFORMATION
Dr. Olya Zahrebelny
636 North Michigan Avenue 3500
Chicago, IL 60610
a. 8934267812

33. BILLING PROVIDER INFO & PH # (312 657 3400
Dr. Olya Zahrebelny
636 North Michigan Avenue 3500
Chicago, IL 60610
a. 8934267812

NUCC Instruction Manual available at www.nucc.org

APPROVED OMB-0938-0999 FORM CMS-1500 (08/05)

The Health Care Finance Administration (HCFA), The Center of Medicaid and Medicare Services (CMS) form 1500

It consists of 33 blocks

The is a medical claim form for individual doctors & practices, nurses, and professionals, including

2.UB04/CMS1450 (Hospital/Technical Claim form):

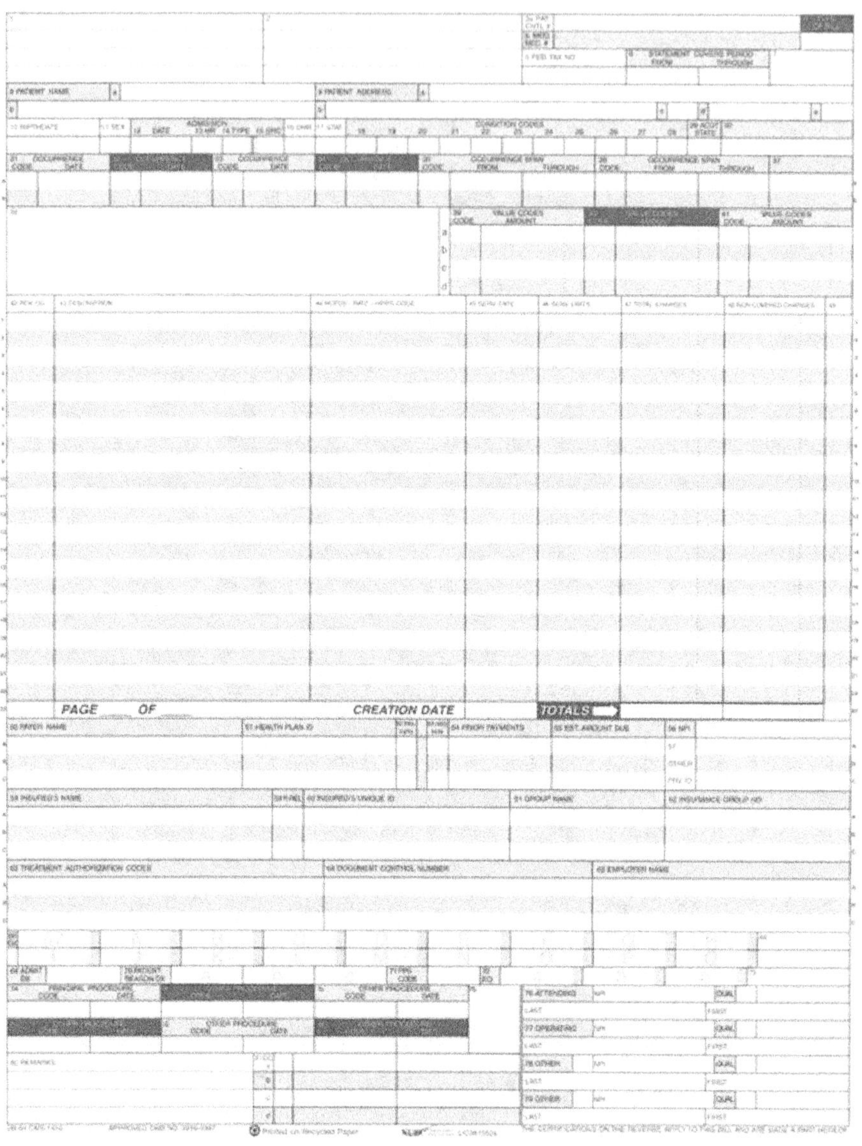

Terminologies:

Place of Service Codes (POS):

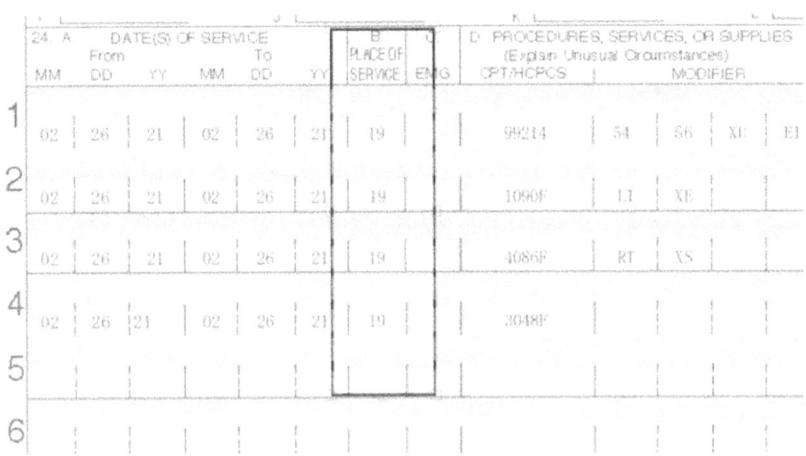

POS means The Service/treatment where rendered

Format: Two-digit numeric (CMS1500 block/box# 24b)

POS codes maintained by The Centers for Medicare & Medicaid Services (CMS)

Examples:

21   Inpatient Hospital

22   On Campus-Outpatient Hospital

23   Emergency Room - Hospital

24   Ambulatory Surgical Center

31   Skilled Nursing Facility

32   Nursing Facility

81   Independent Laboratory etc,...

Type Of Service Codes (TOS):

The type of service value is system generated from the procedure code on the claim and helps describe the procedure code.

Format: Two-digit numeric

Examples:

Transaction Code List - General Type of Service:

01-Medical Care

02-Surgery

03-Consultation

Transaction Code List - Unique Type of Service:

1G-Global Service Radiology

1H-Global Service Laboratory

A-Ambulance

In-Network Provider/Contracted Provider:

The provider who is contracted with the insurance company

Contractual adjustment available

Out of Network Provider/Non-Contracted Provider:

The provider who is not contracted with the insurance company

Contractual adjustment not available

Pre-existing condition:

A medical illness or injury that patient have before started a new health plan

Any service related to this condition will be denied as a PRe-existing condition.A waiting period is available here

Waiting period:

For a patient's pre-existing condition patient have to wait for some time to get the coverage, once the waiting period is over then the claim will be payable by insurance. The duration of the waiting period may vary from company to company. The number of years depends on the patient's age, and what the condition is. During the waiting period the claim never payable.

Capitation:

It is like a prepaid check given to the provider by the insurance company that all the services going to be done by that particular provider will never be paid again and again for each patient visit

Providers are paid for each enrolled patient, or per member per month (PMPM). This is called the capitated rate or capitation premium, or in short form "cap".

Referral number: RAN (Referral Authorization Number) Block# 23

While referring, PCP will generate a "Referral number" which has to be used by the Specialist while billing the claim to insurance if the referral number not entered in the claim form by the Specialist that claims will be denied as missing "Referral number".

Pre/Prior-Authorization: Block# 23

YES   NO
below (24E)   ICD Ind
D   O90.6
22. RESUBMISSION CODE
ORIGINAL REF. NO.
H
23. PRIOR AUTHORIZATION NUMBER
859612374
L
S, SERVICES, OR SUPPLIES
ual Circumstances)   MODIFIER
E DIAGNOSIS POINTER
F $ CHARGES
G DAYS OR UNITS
H EPSDT Family Plan
I ID QUAL
J RENDERING PROVIDER ID. #
54 56 XU E1 1,3   1500 20   1   NPI 123456789
LT XE   1   201 32   3   NPI 123456789

The provider needs to get this from the insurance company before doing certain services.

It is prior approval from the insurance company when the provider is about to perform certain services to the patient, the service is like a high dollar or the service which is going to be a risk to the patient's health condition

Pre-Determination:

Pre-Determination is a process of verifying the patient's eligibility for the date of service to find out whether the service which is going to be done will be covered or not under the patient's health plan. A pre-determination letter or form sent from a medical provider to insurance carrier.

Advance Beneficiary Notice (ABN):

This ABN should give to the patient by the provider before performing the services, It is to inform the patient that if the insurance carrier denies the claim then the patient is responsible to pay the provider.

If the provider missed getting a patient's sign in the ABN form then the provider cannot bill the patient for non-covered services.

Waiver of Liability (WOL) and Advance Beneficiary Notice (ABN):

Both are the same the difference is ABN the term is used for Medicare recipients. Other than Medicare recipients the term is used as Waiver of Liability (WOL)

Assignment of Benefits (AOB):

Patient and Insurance agreement

It is an agreement between the patient and insurance stating the patient agreeing to send payment directly to the provider.

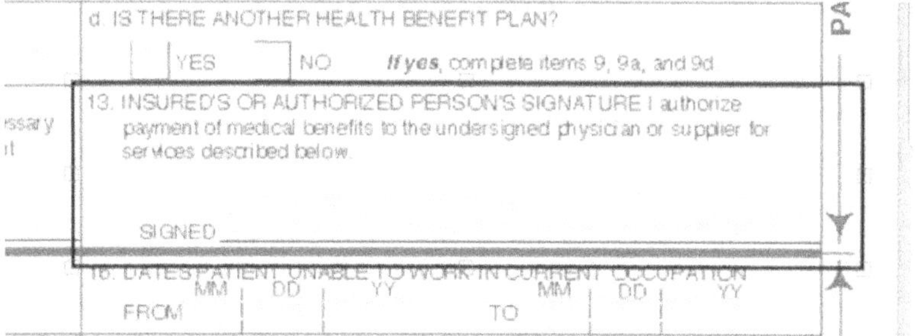

If AOB was not signed by the patient then payment will not be issued to the provider. Payment will be issued directly to the patient.

Release of Information (ROI):

Patient and provider agreement

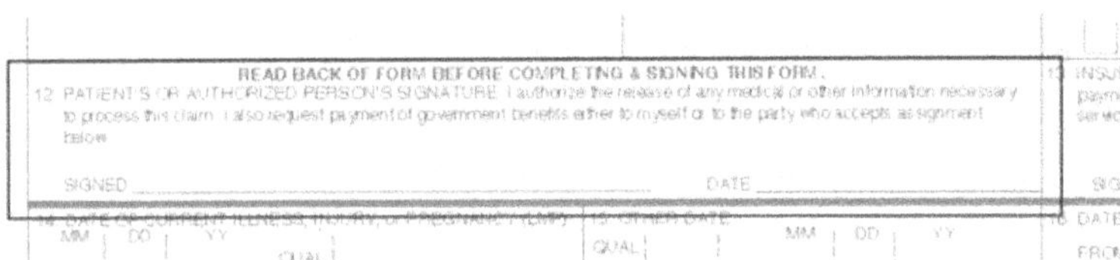

It is an authorization given by the patient to the provider that the provider can share the patient's personal health information with others for billing purposes.

Coordination of Benefits (COB):

To identify which insurance is primary and which insurance is secondary and which one is tertiary.

If the patient has more than one insurance plan, the patient needs to update the COB to both insurances to establish which insurance is primary and which insurance is secondary—the primary payer will pay first and the secondary payer will pay the remaining balance (patient responsibility) after the primary paid.

11. INSURED'S POLICY GROUP OR FECA NUMBER

a. INSURED'S DATE OF BIRTH   SEX
MM | DD | YY
M   F

b. OTHER CLAIM ID (Designated by NUCC)

c. INSURANCE PLAN NAME OR PROGRAM NAME

d. IS THERE ANOTHER HEALTH BENEFIT PLAN?
YES   NO   If yes, complete items 9, 9a, and 9d.

13. INSURED'S OR AUTHORIZED PERSON'S SIGNATURE I authorize payment of medical benefits to the undersigned physician or supplier for services described below.

SIGNED

Refund:

Insurance paid an incorrect payment to the provider

The provider will receive a refund letter from the insurance carrier stating that insurance had paid incorrectly so the provider should return the money to the insurance company

Example: Let the total billed amount of a claim be $100.00 and the specified payment for this is $80.00. The insurance pays $90.00 for the claim. Here $10.00 is paid in excess. Now the insurance requests for a refund of $10.00 which will be done as per the client's specifications.

Recoupment/Take-back (OFFSET):

If the provider has not responded to the refund letter issued by the insurance company then the insurance company will compensate(adjust) that particular amount in the future claims of that provider.

Three Refund letter will be issue to provider, provider need to respond within these three letters, if not then the take back (Recoupment) will be initiated

Example: Let the total billed amount of two claims is $100.00 each and the specified payment for this is $80.00. The insurance pays $90.00 for the first claim. Here $10.00 is paid in excess. Now while making payment for the second claim the insurance pays $70.00 and sets $10.00 as an offset. Now the insurance payment becomes normal as the excess payment had been adjusted off.

Classification of Insurances:

1.   Federal

2.   Semi Federal

3.   Commercial

4.   Liability

5.   Workers Compensation

1.   Federal Insurance:

A.Medicare

B.Medicaid

C.CHAMPUS   - Tricare and CHAMPVA

A.Medicare Insurance:

For Disabled people

Insurance type: Federal health insurance

Administered by: CMS - Centre for Medicaid and Medicare services

Medicare Eligibility:

Must be an American citizen or a permanent resident for at least five continuous years

A person should 65 years and above

Permanently/a Temporarily disabled person.

ESRD - End-Stage Renal Disease

A person who paid Medicare taxes while working for at least 10 years or 40 quarters.

Medicare through Spouse

TFL for Medicare 1 year.

Parts of Medicare:

There are four parts of Medicare: Part A, Part B, Part C, and Part D.

Part A -   Hospital (Inpatient)

Part B - Doctor (outpatient)

Part C - Medicare Advantage

Part D - Prescription drugs

Medicare Part A:

Another name (Hospital Coverage)

Premium-free policy: People don't have to pay a premium for Part A because an individual has already paid 10 years of social service tax under Medicare-covered employment.

However, Part A isn't totally free.

Medicare charges an annual deductible each time admitted to the hospital.

Medicare's Deductible changes every year.

Year:

	2020	2021
INPATIENT HOSPITAL DEDUCTIBLE:	$1408	$1484

Medicare Part A covers:

A.   In-patient hospital care: (Covers Technical component)

In-patient means Patients must stay at the medical facility (which is usually a hospital) for at least one night.

B.   Skilled nursing facility (SNF) care:

They provide the medically necessary services of licensed nurses, physical and occupational therapists, speech pathologists, and audiologists.

C.   Home health care:

Health care services can be given inpatient homes for an illness or injury by trained medical professionals.

D.   Hospice care:

A patient who is at the end stage of their life is treated in this facility.

Medicare Part B:

Another name (Supplemental Medical Insurance)

Not a Premium-free policy. Need to Purchase the policy

In order to purchase Part B coverage, one should have Part A active then only he can purchase Part B.

Medicare Part B covers:

Outpatient Hospital covers professional component (Doctor services)

Durable medical equipment (DME)

Home health services

Ambulance services

Preventive services

Therapy services

Mental health services etc.

Pays for consultation, outpatient Hospital services, and Durable medical equipment

Medicare Part C:

Another name (Medicare Advantage Plan)

Medicare Part C   =   Part A + Part B

Not a Premium-free policy. Need to Purchase the policy

Medicare Advantage plans (PART C) are offered by private insurance companies approved by Medicare.

Medicare Advantage (Part C) plans combine coverage for hospital care (Part A), doctor visits (Part B), and other medical services all in one plan. (Provide all coverage in one plan which includes Part A & B coverage except hospice care, which continues to be provided by Part A).

Medicare Part D:

Another name (Prescription Drug Coverage)

Medicare Part D is offered through private companies.

Not a Premium-free policy. Need to Purchase the policy

Medicare Part A and Part B do not cover prescription drugs one should buy Part D separately along with Part A in order to cover his/her Drug costs.

Two types of coverage:

PDP (Prescription Drug Plan)

MAPD (Medicare Advantage Prescription Drug)

A PDP provides coverage of outpatient prescription drugs

An MAPD provides coverage for out-patient Medicare Part D prescription drugs -and also includes coverage of Medicare Part A (in-patient and hospital coverage) and Medicare Part B (outpatient and physician coverage). An MAPD may also provide supplemental benefits beyond usual Medicare coverage such as vision care, dental care, and more.

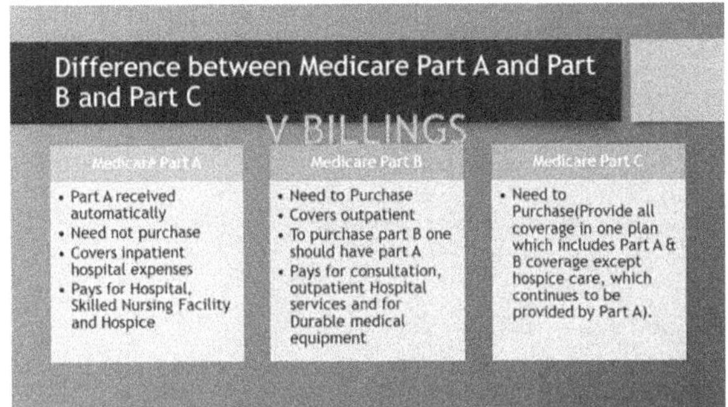

Medicare Cross Over?

Once Medicare completed processing the claim, then automatically Medicare will forward Medicare's EOB to the patient's secondary payer (consecutive payers) for processing. This is called a Medicare-Cross Over claim. Mostly electronic forward happens which is called as Automatic Cross Over".

B.Medicaid Insurance:

For Poor people

Insurance type: Federal health insurance

Administered by: Medicaid is administered by states, according to federal requirements

The people who are below the poverty line (Poor people)

If an annual income is less than the average income of an individual for a month

Points to remember:

Medicaid is a premium free policy

It is administered by state governments and the policy will be renewed on a monthly basis

Medicaid will be the last insurance

No patient responsibility.

Medicaid Spend down charges:

If an individual average income exceeds the Medicaid eligibility slab then the excess amount has to be spent by the individual towards his/her family member's medical expense.

The spend-down will be deducted as deductible from the excess income.

C.CHAMPUS:

Civilian Health and Medical Program of the Uniformed Services

CHAMPUS also called Tricare.

Premium paid policy

It is for Army, Navy, & Military personnel.

They have to register themselves and their dependents in DEERS to get this policy

DEERS: Defense Enrollment Eligibility Reporting System?

DEERS is a computerized database of military sponsors, families, and others worldwide who are entitled to TRICARE and other benefits.

Active-duty and retired service members are automatically registered in DEERS, but they must register their family members and make sure all the information is correct to ensure TRICARE coverage.

D.CHAMPVA:

The Civilian Health and Medical Program of the Department of Veterans Affairs?

A person who served in US Army during war

Premium free policy

If a Veteran who rated temporarily or permanently disabled CHAMPVA provides coverage.

CHAMPVA provides coverage to the spouse or widower and to the children of a Veteran who:

The spouse or child of a Veteran who's been temporarily or permanently disabled for a service-connected disability by a VA regional office, or

The surviving spouse or child of a Veteran who died from a VA-rated service-connected disability, or

The surviving spouse or child of a Veteran who was at the time of death temporarily or permanently disabled from a service-connected disability, or

The surviving spouse or child of a service member who died in the line of duty, not due to misconduct (in most of these cases, family members qualify for TRICARE, not CHAMPVA).

CHAMPVA is always the secondary payer to Medicare.

2.Commercial Insurance:

Commercial Insurance is administered by private insurance companies.

Medicare Advantage Plan:

This is a government plan, is administered by private insurance companies approved by Medicare.

Top Commercial Insurance companies:

United Healthcare

Wellpoint

Aetna

CIGNA

Humana

Centene

Health Net

WellCare Health Plans

Healthspring

Molina Healthcare etc.

3.Workers Compensation insurance:

This is the insurance coverage for the person who got injured
during work.

WC Features:

Dependents are not covered.

Employer (Company) will take care of their employees (Workers)

The company will compensate any kind of loss to its workers
during the work

This plan covers only the disease, infections, or injuries that
are work-related.

The company pays the premium as well as the deductible.

Office of Workers Compensation Programs (OWCP)?

OWCP administers the Federal Employees' Compensation Act (FECA) it provides compensation benefits to workers who got injured during work.

They act as the middle man between Employer, Employee, and WC insurance.

The representatives of this OWCP are called OMBUDSMAN.

4.Liability Insurance:

Liability insurance provides protection against claims resulting from injuries and damage to people and/or property.

Three Important Liability Insurance:

A.Motor Vehicle Accident (MVA)

B.Personal Injury Protection (PIP)

C.Property Damage

A. Motor Vehicle Accident (MVA):

A. Motor Vehicle Accident (MVA):

This insurance pay for the injury or loss that occurred due to a motor vehicle accident. It is mostly state-owned policies.

Various documents supposed to be submitted in order to get payment from insurance, those documents such as:

The accident report from the patient

Medical records from the provider

FIR (First Injury Report) from the police

Witness report from the witnesses.

Coverage for Self, Family, and Designated driver:

B. Personal Injury Protection (PIP):

Personal injury protection (PIP) insurance covers your medical bills and lost wages when you or your passengers are injured in a car accident.

PIP also covers for example: When you are a passenger in someone else's car, or if you are hit by a car while walking or cycling.

It gives coverage to Policy Holder, Dependents, and Designated drivers.

No-Fault Clause/State:

This type of car insurance covers your injuries and the damage you suffer. The fault does not matter in this situation. It is also known as personal injury protection (PIP). PIP claims are typically covered whether or not you are at fault.

12 No-fault states:

Florida, Hawaii, Kansas, Kentucky, Massachusetts, Minnesota, Michigan, New York, New Jersey, North Dakota, Pennsylvania, and Utah.

To find who is at fault will take long and costly court battles in an attempt to reduce this problem the above 12 states are adopted no-fault insurance states.

Collision insurance:

It will typically cover events within a driver's control, or when another vehicle collides with your car.

Collision insurance can also be used toward your rental car in most cases.

Example: The car crashed by hitting a tree while driving.

Comprehensive coverage:

It gives coverage for the damage caused by a natural disaster

It will typically cover events that in the driver's out of control while driving.

Example: A tree branch fell on the car.

Third-Party Coverage:

Bodily Injury Liability (BIL)

Property damage liability (PDL)

Bodily Injury Liability (BIL):

Bodily injury liability insurance pays for injuries you cause to another driver if you are at fault in the accident.

Bodily injury does not cover the medical costs of injuries you may get in the accident. It is considered "third-party" insurance since it only covers other drivers and passengers.

C. Property damage liability (PDL):

This insurance covers the cost of damage caused to others, whether you damaged others' car, house, or any other type of personal property.

Types of Health Plans:

HMO

PPO

POS

EPO

HMO:

Health maintenance organization: Budget-friendly plan.

It is one of the cheapest types of health insurance. It has low premiums and the deductible and fixed copay for doctor visits.

HMO is an individual plan.

In this policy, a PCP (Primary Care Physician) will be allocated.

HMO requires referral# from PCP when patient referred to get treated by a Specialist.

It covers only In-Network benefits, Out of network benefits not available.

POS:

Point-of-Service: Hybrid of HMO and PPO

POS is one of the cheapest types of health insurance. It has low premiums and the deductible and fixed copay for doctor visits.

POS is an individual plan.

PCP (Primary Care Physician) will be allocated in POS,

Requires referral from PCP when patient referred to a Specialist.

Both In-Network benefits and Out of network benefits available.

PPO:

Preferred Provider Organization: A high premium plan but fewer patient responsibilities.

PPO is one of the costliest types of health insurance. It has higher premiums than HMO and POS plan type. Copay and Coinsurance for in-network doctors are low.

PPO is a group policy.

PCP (Primary Care Physician) and Referral not needed.

A patient can directly meet Specialist

Both In-Network benefits and Out of network benefits available.

EPO:

Exclusive Provider Organization: Lower monthly premiums but a higher deductible

If you're looking for lower monthly premiums and are willing to pay a higher deductible when you need health care, you may want to consider an EPO plan.

EPO is a group plan

PCP (Primary Care Physician) and Referral not needed.

A patient can directly meet Specialist

It covers only In-Network benefits. Out-of-network benefits not available.

Table for HMO vs POS vs PPO vs EPO

Benefits of plans	HMO	POS	PPO	EPO
Primary Care Physician (PCP) required?	Yes	Yes	No	No
Out of network Coverage?	No	Yes	Yes	No
Referral needed?	Yes	Yes	No	No
Premiums Cost?	Low	Medium	High	Lower than PPO

Arrangement of Insurances:

Primary Insurance:

The insurance company pays first.

Secondary Insurance:

This pays balance after the primary insurance which may include co-insurance, deductible, and non-covered under primary.

Tertiary Insurance:

If secondary insurance denies the claim for some reason then the bill can be submitted to tertiary.

Deductible:

A deductible is usually a fixed dollar amount that the patient has to pay from his pocket before the insurance starts to cover Depending on the insurance plan the deductible can range from $0 up to thousands of dollars.   Generally, Plans with lower monthly premiums have a higher Deductible.   Medicare's Deductible changes every year.

Year:
2020   2021

INPATIENT HOSPITAL DEDUCTIBLE: $1408 $1484

Co-Pay:

A co-payment is the smallest fixed amount for a covered service, paid by a patient to the provider before receiving the specified service.

Generally, Plans with lower monthly premiums have a higher copay.

Co-payments such as $5, $10, $15, $20 etc.,

Co-Insurance:

Coinsurance is a portion or % of the medical cost that patient pays after the patient's deductible has been met.

Coinsurance is a way of saying that patient and the patient's insurance carrier each pay a share of eligible costs that add up to 100 %.

For example, Insurance pays 80 % and the remaining 20% is patient responsibility as coinsurance

How claim will process in terms of benefits?

Out of pocket maximum/limit

(Deductibles + Co-payments + Co-insurances)

Most of the patients have to pay for covered services in a plan year. After spending this amount on deductibles, co-payments, and co-insurance for in-network care services, the patient's health plan pays 100% of the costs of covered benefits

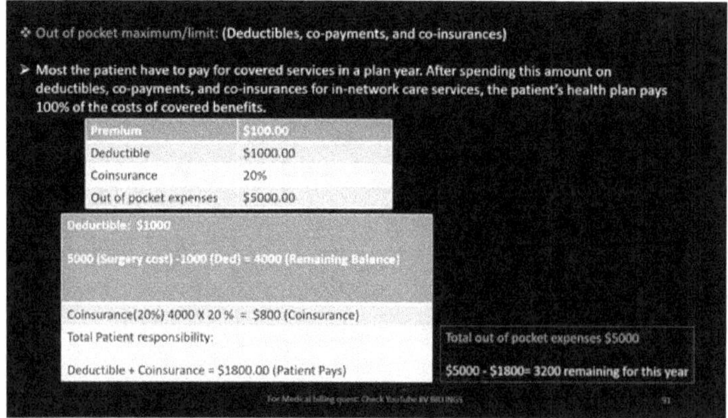

Stop-loss clause:

(Same as Deductible)

Stop-loss insurance is also known as excess insurance,

It is a product that provides protection against catastrophic or unpredictable losses.

It is purchased by employers who have decided to self-fund their employee benefit plans but do not want to assume 100% of the liability for losses arising from the plans.

Under a stop-loss policy, the insurance company becomes liable for losses that exceed certain limits called deductibles.

For example: If an employer elects that their maximum liability per person on their benefits plan for that policy year be $10,000 and a specific claimant exceeds that liability and their total claims are $10,200, the stop-loss policy will reimburse them for claims over that amount, the $200.

There are two types of Self-funded insurance:

Specific stop-loss (Individual):

Covers excessive claims for an employee, his or her spouse, and children on an individual basis.

Aggregate (Entire group):

Covers claims for an entire group when its claims exceed a specified amount determined by the insurance carrier over the course of a year.

Timely filing limit (TFL):

It is a time limit given by the insurance company to the provider to submit a claim for processing. If the provider failed to send a claim within the specified time limit then the insurance company will deny the claim as "Late filing".

The time limit differs for each insurance company.

List of timely filing limit for major insurance companies:

ARP	15 Months
Advantage Care	6 Months
Advantage Freedom	2 Years

Aetna timely filing	120 Days
Ameri health ADM Local 360	1 Year
American Life and Health	12 Months
American Progressive	1 Year
Amerigroup	90 Days for Par Providers or 12 months for Non-Par Providers
Amerihealth ADM TPA	1 Year
AmeriHealth NJ & DE	60 Days
Arbazo	180 Days
Bankers Life	15 Months

BCBS timely filing for Commercial/Federal	180 Days from Initial Claims or if its secondary 60 Days from Primary EOB
BCBS COVERKIDS	120 Days
BCBS Florida timely filing	12 Months
BeechStreet	90 Days

Benefit Trust Fund	1 year from Medicare EOB
Blue Advantage HMO	180 Days
Blue Cross PPO	1 Year
Blue Essential	180 Days
Blue Premier	180 Days
Blue Shield timely filing	1 Year
Blue shield High Mark	60 Days
Cigna timely filing (Commercial Plans)	90 Days for Par Providers or 180 Days for Non Par Providers
Cigna HealthSprings (Medicare Plans)	120 Days
Citrus	1 Year
Coventry	180 Days
Evercare	60 Days
First Health	3 Months
GHI	1 Year
Great West	90 Days

Great West	15 Months
Healthcare Partners	90 Days
Healthnet HMO	90 Days
Healthnet PPO	120 Days
Horizon NJ Plus	365 Days
Humana	180 Days for Physicians
Humana	27 Months
ILWU	3 Years
Keystone Health Plan East	60 Days
Local 831 Health	1 year
Magna Care	6 Months
Marilyn Electro IND. Benefit Fund	1 Year
Medicaid	95 Days
Medicare	1 Year
Mega Life and Health	15 Months

Memorial IPA	90 Days
Monarch IPA	90 Days
Mutual of Omaha	1 year
NASI	2 Years
Omnicare IPA	90 Days
One Healthplan	15 Months
Operating Engineers	1 Year
Pacific Health Care IPA	90 Days
Pioneer Medical Group	60 Days
Polk Community Health Care	180 Days
Prospect Medical Group	90 Days
PUP	180 Days
Quality Health Plan	1 Year
Secure Hoizons	90 Days
Sun	180 Days

Tricare	12 Months
UFCW	1 year
UHC Community	120 Days
Unicare	24 Months
United Health Care - UHC COMMERCIAL	90 Days
Veterans Admin	90 Days
Vista	120 Days
Wellcare	180 Days
Zenith	1 year
Medi-Cal	1 year from the date of service 7-9 month = 75% of allowed amount 10-12 month = 50% of allowed amount
Medicare	12 months from date of service

Pre-Audit/ Pre-Edit:

A pre-audit is preliminary work conducted by an auditor here auditor will check for basic error which was not recognized by the clearinghouse.

Sometimes clearing houses might not know the update made recently on changes in Dx, CPT, Modifier, etc. These updates are all recognized in Pte-Audit and the claim will be rejected in the initial stage and returned to the provider office.

Claim adjudication:

Once the claim reached the insurance company, a specific department called the Claim adjudication department analyzes the claim and decides to pay the claim in full, deny the claim, or reduce the amount paid to the provider.

Five steps in the claim adjudication process:

The initial processing review.

The automatic review.

The manual review.

The payment determination.

The payment.

Five steps in the adjudication process:

1. The initial processing review:

Incorrect patient name, Incorrect POS, Wrong DOS, Invalid or missing DX, Wrong plan or subscriber identification number, Mismatch of service, and patient's gender

2. The automatic review:

Patient Eligibility, Absence or invalid authorization and pre-certification, Duplicate claims are submitted or not, TFL exceeded or not, Invalid CPT or DX code, The services are medically necessary or not.

3. The manual review:

Medical claim examiners check the claims manually. Here compare the medical documentation with the claims.

4. The payment determination:

Three types of payment determinations:

 - **If the payer determines the claim is reimbursable**

 - **If the payer determines that the claim is non-reimbursable**

 - **When the billed amount is too high the claims can down-code to a lower level as deemed appropriate.**

5.   The payment:

Payment issued to the medical care provider for the rendered services. Payment can be sent through EFT, Paper Check, Credit card transaction, etc., After the payment process, an EOB will be issued to the provider as well as the Patient.

Explanation of benefits:

Insurance will send to the provider and patient.

After the adjudication process, the decision taken during that process is communicated to provider and patient using the statement called EOB

The most important thing to keep remember is an EOB is NOT a bill.

EOB contains:

Member information

Patient account number

Service codes:

Total amount:

Not covered amount:

Reason code description:

Covered by plan

Provider name

Claim number

Date of service

Deductibles and Co-payments:

Total net payment:

Total Patient Responsibility:

Checks Details: Payee's name, check number, and check amount.

EOB sample:

See how your benefits are working for you with this easy-to-understand document that shows you the costs associated with the medical care you've received.

When a claim is filed under your CIGNA benefits plan, you get an Explanation of Benefits (EOB). Because we know health care expenses can be confusing, we've simplified the language and summarized the most important information about the claim.

The Summary page gives an overview of how your benefits are working for you – quickly see what was submitted, what's been paid, and what you owe.

Date of service and health care professional are both listed for easier reference.

If your health accounts paid part of your expenses, you'll see what's been paid and remaining balances.

The amount you owe does not reflect any amount you may have already paid.

This reflects the total value of your plan – the amount you saved by visiting an in-network health care professional or facility, and the amount paid by your plan.

The Claims Detail page follows the Glossary page. Here, you'll find:

The dollar amount and percentage CIGNA paid toward the covered amount, minus any copay/deductible you're responsible for.

The portion of covered expenses you're responsible for paying. For example, if your CIGNA plan covers 90% of the covered amount, you pay the remaining 10%.

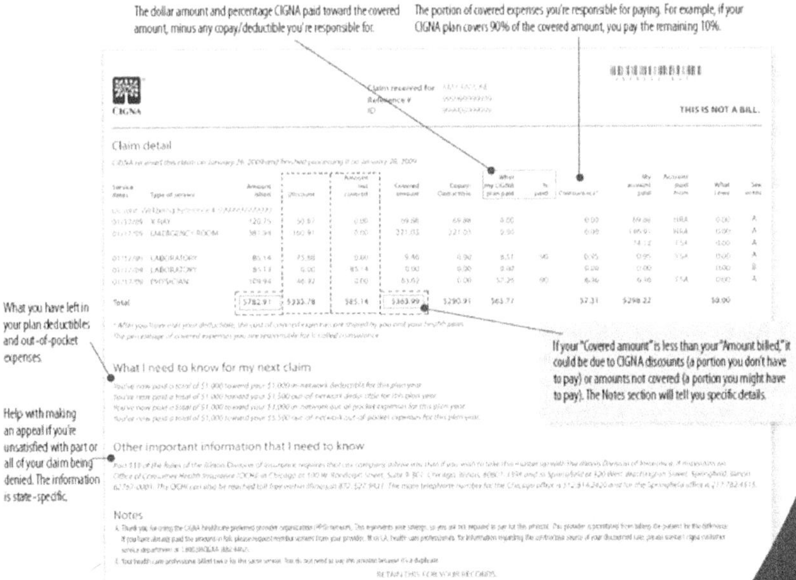

What you have left in your plan deductibles and out-of-pocket expenses.

Help with making an appeal if you're unsatisfied with part or all of your claim being denied. The information is state-specific.

If your "Covered amount" is less than your "Amount billed," it could be due to CIGNA discounts (a portion you don't have to pay) or amounts not covered (a portion you might have to pay). The Notes section will tell you specific details.

Payment Posting:

After insurance completes the claim processing, the payment will be issued along with an Explanation of Benefits (EOB) to provider pay to address. The payment will receive in many ways paper check, eft, credit card, etc, Once the payment is received successfully by referencing the received EOB that payment details will be posted in the patient account.

If the payment posted correctly and there is no other balance in that patient account that particular claim will be zeroed out which means the claim was completed.

Billed Amount:

The amount charged by the provider for the service rendered to a patient.

CES, OR SUPPLIES umstances) MODIFIER	E DIAGNOSIS POINTER	F $ CHARGES	G DAYS OR UNITS	H EPSDT Family Plan	I ID QUAL		J RENDERING PROVIDER ID #
56 XU EI	1.3	1500 20	i		NPI		123456789
XE	1	201 32	3		NPI		123456789
XS	2				NPI		123456789
	4				NPI		123456789
					NPI		
					NPI		

27 ACCEPT ASSIGNMENT? (For govt. claims, see back)	28 TOTAL CHARGE	29 AMOUNT PAID	30 Rsvd for NUCC
YES NO	$ 1701 52	$ 0 00	

CR INFORMATION

33. BILLING PROVIDER INFO & PH # ( )

V BILLINGS CLINIC
51 Hollywood Pkway

Allowed Amount:

It is the maximum amount allowed by the insurance company for the service rendered

by the provider. This amount is based on the provider and payer contract which was

discussed and listed in the provider fee-Schedule.

Fee-Schedule:

It is a list of charges for health care services. Providers keep fee schedules in their offices to specify the amount of compensation they want for providing selected services.

Example:

Labor Epidural codes 01967 & 01968 are reimbursed at a flat rate.

Fee-Schedule sample Reference: mmis.georgia.gov

Code	Modifier	Rate Amount
01967	AA	$ 248.50
	QK	$ 82.83
	QY	$ 82.83
	QX	$165.66
	QZ	$ 246.02

Code	Modifier	Rate Amount
01968	AA	$ 400.00
	QK	$133.33
	QY	$133.33
	QX	$266.66
	QZ	$ 396.00

Contractual Adjustment:

The contract between provider and insurance agrees to discount (Write off).

The difference between what the provider billed and what the insurance plan allows. The

patient is not responsible. The provider should write off the difference amount.

Claim detail

CIGNA received this claim on January 26, 2009 and fi...

provider wirte-off/ contractual adjust

Service dates	Type of service	Amount billed	Discount	Amount not covered	Covered amount	Copay/ Deductible	What my CIGNA plan paid	% paid	Coinsurance*	My account paid	Account paid from	What I owe	See notes
Dr. John Wellbeing Reference # 9999999999999													
01/17/09	X-RAY	120.75	50.87	0.00	69.88	69.88	0.00		0.00	69.88	HRA	0.00	A
01/17/09	EMERGENCY ROOM	381.94	160.91	0.00	221.03	221.03	0.00		0.00	146.91	HRA	0.00	A
										74.12	FSA	0.00	A
01/17/09	LABORATORY	85.14	75.68	0.00	9.46	0.00	8.51	90	0.95	0.95	FSA	0.00	A
01/17/09	LABORATORY	85.14	0.00	85.14	0.00	0.00	0.00		0.00	0.00		0.00	B
01/17/09	PHYSICIAN	109.94	46.32	0.00	63.62	0.00	57.26	90	6.36	6.36	FSA	0.00	A
Total		$782.91	$333.78	$85.14	$363.99	$290.91	$65.77		$7.31	$298.22		$0.00	

** After you have met your deductible, the cost of covered expenses are shared by you and your health plan. The percentage of covered expenses you are responsible for is called coinsurance.*

Important short forms used in medical billing:

EOB - Explanation of benefits

COB -Co-ordination of Benefits

MSP - Medicare as a Secondary Payer

POS - Place of service

TOS - Type of Service

DOS - Date of service

ICD - 9 -International Statistical Classification of Diseases and Related Health Problems-9th Edition

CPT - Current Procedural Terminology

HCPCS - Healthcare Common Procedure Coding System

HIPAA Health Insurance Portability and Accountability Act

RBRVS - The Resource-Based Relative Value Scale

RVU - Relating Value Unit

CHAMPUS - Civilian Health and Medical Program of the Uniformed Services

CHAMPVA - Civilian Health and Medical Program for the Veteran Administration

NCCI: National Correct Coding Initiative

ESRD - End-Stage Renal Disease

FICA - Federal Insurance Contributions Act

HICN - Health Insurance Claim Number

COBRA - Consolidated Omnibus Budget Reconciliation Act

EGHP - Employer Group Health Plan

UCR - Usual, customary, and reasonable

PCP - Primary care physician

HMO - Health Maintenance Organization

PPO - Preferred Provider Organization

TPA - Third Party Administrators

HIPAA- Health Insurance Portability and Accountability
Act

All short forms in Alphabetic orders:

ABN: Advance Beneficiary Notice of Non-coverage

ADA: American Dental Association

ALJ: Administrative Law Judge

AMA: American Medical Association

ANSI: American National Standards Institute

ASA: American Society of Anesthesiologists

ASC: Ambulatory Surgical Center

BBA: Balanced Budget Act

CAH: Critical Access Hospital

CCI: refer to NCCI

CCN: Correspondence Control Number

CDE: Certified Diabetic Educators

CLIA: Clinical Laboratory Improvement Amendments

CMD: Contractor Medical Director

CMHC: Community Mental Health Center

CMN: Certificate of Medical Necessity

CMR: Comprehensive Medical Review

CMS: The Centers for Medicare & Medicaid Services

CNM: Certified Nurse Midwife

CNMW: Certified Nurse Midwife

CNS: Certified Nurse Specialist

CPT: Current Procedural Terminology

CRD: Chronic Renal Disease

CRNA: Certified Registered Nurse Anesthetist

CWF: Common Working File

DHHS: Department of Health & Human Services

DME: Durable Medical Equipment

DOB: Date of Birth

DOS: Date of Service

DX: Diagnosis/Diagnoses

ECF: Extended Care Facility

EDI: Electronic Data Interchange

EIN: Employer Identification Number (Tax ID)

EKG: Electrocardiogram

E/M: Evaluation and Management

EOB: Explanation of Benefits

ERA: Electronic Remittance Advice

ESRD: End-Stage Renal Disease

FDA: Food and Drug Administration

HICN: Health Insurance Claim Number

HIPAA Health Insurance Portability and Accountability Act

HMO: Health Maintenance Organization

HPSA: Health Professional Shortage Area

ICD-9-CM: Internal Classification of Diseases-9th Edition

ICU: Intensive Care Unit

LMRP: Local Medical Review Policy

MSN: Medicare Summary Notice

MSP: Medicare Secondary Payer

NCCI: National Correct Coding Initiative

NON-PAR: Non-Participating Provider

NPI: National Provider Identifier

POS: Place of Service or Point of Service Option

PPO: Preferred Provider Organization

PQRI: Physician Quality Reporting Initiative

RA: Remittance Advice

SNF: Skilled Nursing Facility

SSN: Social Security Number

TOS: Type of Service

Denials / AR Scenarios

AUTHORIZATION:missing/invalid:

(BLOCK 23)

Questions to probe with Payer Rep:

Claim received date?

Claim denied date?

Check system for auth is available or not if found give that to the rep and reprocess

Check claim image if auth# found in Block#23 give that to rep for reprocess

If auth# not found in any way, ask the rep if Retro authorization is possible or not? If retro auth is possible then ask the procedure to get retro auth.

If retro auth not possible then ask for appeal address and timely filing limit for appeal

Claim# and Call reference# Thank you.

REFERRAL missing/invalid :(BLOCK 23)

RENDERING PROVIDER:**A provider who provides actual service.**

REFERRING PROVIDER/Primary Care Physician/ Family Doctor: A provider who provides initial service.

Questions to probe with Payer Rep:

Claim received date?

Claim denied date?

Check system for referral is available or not if found give that to rep and reprocess

Check claim image if referral# found in Block#23 give that to rep for reprocess

If referral# not found in anyway, ask rep what is PCP (primary care physician) name and PCP phone# and get the corrected claim address and time filing limit

Claim# and Call reference#Thank you.

PPO & EPO plan doesn't require a referral, if the patient plan is PPO & EPO ask the rep to reprocess.

BUNDLE/INCLUSIVE/EXCLUSIVE:

First, understand what is inclusive: Inclusive/Bundled is a payment method that combines minor surgeries with principal procedures when performed together.

Example: If an x-ray for both right shoulder and left shoulder was taken on the same day (DOS) and we billed with CPT code 73030 (both right and left side). Again, there is a need to take another x-ray on the left side so we took a separate x-ray and billed CPT code 73020. In this case, we will receive denial stating 73020 x-rays for the left shoulder have already included with 73030.

Questions to probe with Payer Rep:

Claim received date?

Claim denied date?

Ask the rep to which Primary CPT code it was included with, get that Primary CPT code from the rep, and verify that primary CPT code was billed on the same claim or not, if not then ask on which DOS this primary CPT code was billed with?

Can we send the corrected claim with the appropriate modifier? If yes what is the corrected claim mailing address and TFL? if the corrected claim not possible then ask what is the appeal address and appeal TFL?

Claim# and Call reference#

Thank you.

***Note: If the claim billed with Modifier "59" then ask the rep to REPROCESS since this is "Distinct Procedural Service" - Under certain circumstances, the physician may need to indicate that a procedure or service was distinct or independent from other services performed on the same day.

Timely Filing Limit exceeded (TFL):

Payer have some time limit to submit the claim if provider missed to submit within that time limit claim will be denied as exceeded the time limit. Time limit differs from insurance companies.

Questions to probe with Payer Rep

Claim received date?

Claim denied date?

Ask rep what is the normal TFL?

Check the received date, if the claim received within the TFL specified by the rep, then ask for reprocess

If the received date was exceeded the TFL then ask for the appeal address and appeal TFL

Appeal with proof of timely filing limit (POTFL)

Claim# and Call reference#Thank you.

***Note: POFTL can be anything that we have when we had submitted the claim within a time frame Usually, POFTL will be a clearinghouse report.

Primary paid more than the secondary allowed amount:

Questions to probe with Payer Rep:

Claim received date?

Claim denied date?

Ask rep what is the secondary allowed amount?

Check the primary paid amount in primary EOB, if primary paid more than secondary allowed then adjust the claim, If primary paid is less than secondary allowed then ask the rep to reprocess.

Claim# and Call reference# Thank you.

Primary EOB missing:

Questions to probe with Payer Rep:

Claim received date?

Claim denied date?

Check system for primary eob, if we have primary eob then ask the mailing address and TFL to resubmit the claim with primary eob

If we are not having primary eob also we don't know who is primary, then ask the rep about primary payer details like primary payer name, primary payer member id#, and primary payer phone number#

Claim# and Call reference#

Thank you.

Medically not Necessary:

Questions to probe with Payer Rep:

Claim received date?

Claim denied date?

Ask rep why this is medically not a necessity?

Ask rep can we submit a corrected claim by changing the Diagnosis code? If yes ask corrected claim mailing address and TFL. If not possible then ask for an appeal address and TFL.

Claim# and Call reference#

Thank you.

***Note:

Medically not necessity usually denotes Dx corrections so if the corrected claim is possible, we can resubmit by changing the Dx code. If a corrected claim not possible we need to appeal with complete medical records to show how medically necessary this service was. ***For Medicare claims ask the rep for any LCD/NCD# available?

Co-ordination of Benefits (COB) update:

COB: If the patient more than one insurance then the patient needs to update the COB to show who is primary and who is secondary and who is tertiary.

Questions to probe with Payer Rep:

Claim received date?

Claim denied date?

Ask rep, when the Patient last updated the COB?

Check if the DOS is lies within 1 year from the last updated date then ask for reprocess (reprocess only a possibility, not a compulsion)

Ask rep did they send a letter to the member regarding the COB update? If yes ask how many letters sent so far and get those dates also ask did, they received any response from the member, if not ask to send another letter (Mostly 3 letters possible)

If 3 letters sent out already then ask how the member can update it (mostly rep will provide member service dept phone#, here member can call this number to update the COB)

Ask the rep can we bill the patient?

Claim# and Call reference#

Thank you.

Pre-existing condition:

What is Pre-existing condition?

A medical illness or injury that you have before a patient starts a new health care plan.

Questions to probe with Payer Rep:

Claim received date?

Claim denied date?

Ask rep, is there any waiting period?

Get the waiting period start and end date

If the DOS lies between the start and end date of the waiting period, then ask did they send any letter to member, if not ask to send a letter regarding the pre-existing denial

Now ask can we bill the patient?

If the DOS is not lies between the start and end date of the waiting period, then ask the rep to reprocess.

Claim# and Call reference#

Thank you.

Waiting period:

It is the period during which a member cannot claim some medical benefits.

Member should wait for a specified amount of time before making a claim.

The duration of the waiting period may vary from company to company.

Non covered service:

Questions to probe with Payer Rep:

Claim received date?

Claim denied date?

Ask rep, is non covered under patient plan or provider contract?

If under the patient's plan then ask what is non-covered in that? and ask can we bill the patient?

If under provider's contract then ask what is non-covered in that? Then we need to write off.

Claim# and Call reference# Thank you.

***Note:

If a claim denied under the patient plan, check if the patient has secondary insurance then we can bill to secondary insurance.

Before billing the claim to Secondary need to verify eligibility for the secondary payer.

If no other insurance found then bill patient

Patient policy terminated/Patient coverage terminated:

Questions to probe with Payer Rep:

Claim received date?

Claim denied date?

Ask rep, what is the patient policy effective and termed date.

If the DOS is lies between the effective and termed date then ask the rep to reprocess

f the DOS is not lies between the effective and termed date then ask the rep "is there any other active policy found on this DOS" if found ask that new policy details like member id#, policy effective, and termed date.

If no other active policy found then and ask can we bill the patient?

Claim# and Call reference#

Thank you.

Check for other insurance is available or not if other insurance found then check eligibility for that insurance and if the patient is active for that insurance then make it as primary and resubmit the claim.

Claim denied for Global:

Questions to probe with Payer Rep:

Claim received date?

Claim denied date?

Ask rep what is the DOS that the main surgery performed?

Ask the rep what is the Global period?

If the DOS lies within the Global period then ask can we send a corrected claim with an appropriate modifier? If yes, then get corrected claim address and TFL, if the corrected claim not possible the ask for the appeal address and TFL.

If the DOS is not lies within the Global period then ask the rep to reprocess

Claim# and Call reference#Thank you.

When the DOS lies in the Global period range then it should be provider write off

Before write off assign it to the coding team for clarification because we can send a corrected claim with a modifier to indicate this service is independent of main surgery.

Maximum benefits met:

Questions to probe with Payer Rep:

Claim received date?

Claim denied date?

Ask rep patient is enrolled in a dollar plan or visit plan?

If it is under a dollar plan then ask how many dollars is allowed for this patient for a calendar year? Also, ask how much met in that so far? (If balance dollars is available ask to reprocess)

If it is under a visit plan then ask how many visits are allowed for this patient for a calendar year? Also, ask how much met in that so far? (If balance visits are available ask to reprocess)

Ask rep on which DOS patient has met the maximum benefits limit

Now ask can we bill the patient?

Claim# and Call reference#Thank you.

***Note:If the patient has active secondary insurance on DOS then bill the claim to secondary.

If no other active insurance found on DOS then bill the patient.

Duplicate:

How duplicate happen: If two claims are submitted with the same information like (Same DX, CPT, MODIFIER, BILLED AMOUNT, PROVIDER information, etc,). If any one of these details is differing then you can inform the differences you found rep and ask to reprocess the duplicate claim.

Questions to probe with Payer Rep:

Claim received date?

Claim denied date?

First, ask the rep whether this claim was received as a new claim or a corrected claim? (mostly it will come as a new claim, suppose if rep checked and found it was received as a corrected claim then the denial is incorrect so ask the rep to reprocess)

Verify with the rep all these details are the same or not (DX, CPT, MODIFIER, BILLED AMOUNT, PROVIDER information, etc), if it is different ask to reprocess

If it is the same then ask about the original claim status

Get both Original Claim# and Duplicate claim# and then Call reference#

Thank you.

***Note:

If the original claim was paid then get the paid status, if it is in the process then allow some more days, if it is denied for some other reason then question about that specific denial scenario.

Provider is Out of Network:

Sometimes provider contracts with insurance may be terminated at that time provider will be considered as out of network.

 Questions to probe with Payer Rep:

Claim received date?

Claim denied date?

Ask the rep the date "from when the provider is out of network"?

Ask the rep "may I know the patient policy plan type"? (HMO, PPO, POS, or EPO)? if the patient plan is PPO ask the rep to reprocess.

If the patient plan type is other than PPO then ask the rep can we bill the patient?

Claim# and Call reference#

Thank you.

Dx code is inconsistent with CPT code:

Questions to probe with Payer Rep:

Claim received date?

Claim denied date?

Ask the rep "may I know which Dx code is inconsistent with CPT?

now check the patient's entire claims history if this same CPT and DX code combination has received any payment previously?

If payment received previously with the same CPT and Dx code combination then inform the rep about that previous paid DOS and ask the rep to reprocess this denied claim

If no payment was received previously then ask "Can we submit a corrected claim with the appropriate Dx code?" If yes then get the corrected claim mailing address and TFL. If no then get the appeal address and TFL.

Claim# and Call reference# Thank you.

***Note:Claim assigned to a coding team to review once response received with correct Dx code then send corrected claim

Modifier is inconsistent with CPT code:

Questions to probe with Payer Rep:

Claim received date?

Claim denied date?

Ask the rep "may I know why this modifier is inconsistent with CPT"?

now check the patient's entire claims history if this same CPT and modifier combination has received any payment previously?

If payment received previously with the same CPT and modifier combination then inform the rep about that previous paid DOS and ask the rep to reprocess this denied claim

If no payment was received previously then ask "Can we submit a corrected claim with the appropriate modifier?" If yes then get the corrected claim mailing address and TFL. If no then get the appeal address and TFL.

Claim# and Call reference#Thank you.

***Note:Claim assigned to a coding team to review once response received with correct Modifier then send corrected claim

Frequency or Units exceeded:

Questions to probe with Payer Rep:

Claim received date?

Claim denied date?

Ask the rep "how many units are allowed for this CPT code"?

Ask the rep "units are allowed per day or per calendar year"? (mention in notes that allowed units given by rep)

Check your claim if we have billed more than the allowed units then ask the rep "can we send an appeal"?

If appeal possible then get the appeal mailing address and TFL (Appeal with medical records)

Claim# and Call reference#

Thank you.

***Note:

Appeal with medical records

Non-Denials / AR Scenarios

Offset Claim Processed towards Offset:

It is an adjustment when the insurance company previously paid incorrectly to the provider (mostly it is like an over-payment)

The offset can be taken on different patients under that provider.

Questions to probe with Payer Rep:

Claim received date?

Claim processed date?

Ask the rep "may I know the reason, why it was applied towards offset?

Ask the rep may I know the allowed amount for this claim?

Ask the rep "is there any patient responsibilities on this claim"?(Get the pt resp to bill patient)

Ask the rep "how much the Offset amount"?

Ask the rep "offset made on same patient account or different patient account"?

Ask the rep "can I get the over-paid patient account#, check#, DOS & CPT code"?

Ask the rep "could you please fax the EOB? if not then ask to send the EOB to the provider's mailing address.

Claim# and Call reference#

Thank you.

***Note:

Once the EOB received then send it for posting.

Capitation Claim Processed towards Capitation:

It is like a prepaid check given to the provider by the insurance company that all the services going to be done by that particular provider will never be paid again and again for each patient visit.

Questions to probe with Payer Rep:

Claim received date?

Claim processed date?

Ask the rep "may I know the Capitation period"? (Get the start and end date of Cap period)

If the DOS is lies between the capitation period then this claim should be a write-off.

If the DOS is not lies between the capitation period then ask the rep to reprocess

If the insurance is Medicare/Medicaid the get the managed care plan details like payer name and member id (claim need to resubmit to managed care plan)

Claim# and Call reference#

Thank you.

***Note:
For managed care plan(MCO/HMO):

Medicaid has the same member id so we can submit the claim to MCO/HMO under the same member id

Medicare has a different member id so need to find out the correct member id by calling the MCO/HMO.

Other payers:
The claim needs to adjust with client approval

Claim not on file:

Questions to probe with Payer Rep:

If the rep says no claim on file, then ask

What is the correct mailing address and electronic payer id?

What is the timely filing limit to submit the claim?

Ask the rep "may I know the patient policy effective date and termed date"?(sometimes patient policy already termed at that time claims cannot be reached to the payer)

***Note:

If a patient policy is not active then contact the patient for active payer information.

If no active payer on this DOS then bill the patient

***Very important point for Freshers to remember:

Please don't ask the claim#

Claim is still in process:

Questions to probe with Payer Rep:

Claim received date?

What is the normal processing time?

If exceeded the normal processing time then ask the rep "may I the reason for delay"

How many days it will take to complete?

Claim# and Call reference#

Thank you.

***Note:

Allow some more days in order to process

Claim Paid:

Questions to probe with Payer Rep:

Claim received date?

Claim paid date?

Ask the rep "what is the allowed amount"?

Ask the rep "how much the claim paid"?

Ask the rep "is there any patient responsibility"

Ask the rep "Paid thru Check or EFT"

Ask the rep "may I know the check#"

Ask the rep "the check is single or bulk?"

Ask the rep "what is the bulk amount"

Ask the rep "check paid to which address"

Ask the rep "Do you have a cash date" (if the paid date is more than 30 days then ask for cash date, if not more than 30 days don't ask)

Ask the rep "Could you fax the eob"

Claim# and Call reference#

Thank you.

***Note:

For EFT transaction get the transaction id#, don't ask the EFT paid to address, since EFT is an online transaction

If the check sent to a different address ask the rep to stop the check and reissue a new check to the correct address (you have to provide the correct pay to address)

Check paid to correct address but no cash date even the paid date is more than 30 days then ask to do "check trace".

Deductible Claim processed towards Deductible:

A deductible is usually a fixed dollar amount that the patient has to pay from his pocket before the insurance starts to cover.

Depending on the insurance plan the deductible can range from $0 up to thousands of dollars.

Generally, plans with lower monthly premiums have a higher Deductible.

Questions to probe with Payer Rep:

Claim received date?

Ask the rep "may I know the allowed amount"

Ask the rep" how much is applied towards deductible"

Ask the rep "may I know the patient's annual deductible amount"

Ask the rep "the claim processed to in-network deductible or out-of-network deductible"

Ask the rep "may I know how much patient has met in annual deductible as of this DOS"

Claim# and Call reference#

Thank you.

***Note: Once the EOB received then send it for posting.

If the patient has a secondary payer on DOS then submit the claim to secondary.

If no other payer available on DOS then bill the claim to the patient once the deductible posted

MOCK CALLS

MOCK-NON-COVERED SERVICE:

1.Sandy: Thanks for calling this is Sandy, how may I help you?

James: Hi, my name is James, I am calling for Doctor's office and I would like to check the claim status for a patient

Sandy: Which Doctor's office you calling for?

James: I am calling for General Orthopaedic associates

Sandy: What is your telephone number?

James: My telephone# is 800-999-9999

Sandy: What is the patient's SSN (social security number)?

James: The SSN is 123-456-789

Sandy: Could you please hold for a moment so that I can pull the patient records?

James: Yes, please!

Sandy: What is the patient's name and DOB?

2.James: The patient name is Linda Far and DOB is 11-26-1995

Sandy: What is the DOS you checking for?

James: The DOS is 12-10-2020

Sandy: What is the billed amount on this claim?

James: The billed amount is $150.00

Sandy: Could you please hold for a moment so that I can pull up the claim?

James: Yes Of course!

Sandy: Thanks for been on hold James the claim was denied?

James: Okay may I know the claim received date?

Sandy: The claim was received on 12-15-2020

3.James: And what is the denial date?

Sandy: The denial date is 12-22-2020

James: May I know the reason for the denial?

Sandy: Claim was denied for non-covered service.

James: Non-covered as per patient plan or provider contract?

Sandy: Non covered as per Patient plan and the patient plan does not cover OON benefits

James: What plan does the patient have? Sandy!

Sandy: Let me find that James?

James: Okay

Sandy: James the patient plan is HMO

4.James: Okay Sandy thanks for that information, could you please Fax the eob?

Sandy: Yes, what is your FAX#?

James: The fax# is 842-543-6789 and you can put attention as my name JAMES

Sandy: Okay James the fax request has been submitted and it will be received within a day

James: Thanks Sandy what is the claim?

Sandy: The claim is 884455

James: Is there any reference # for this call?

Sandy: Yes, James it is 0285

James: Thank you so much Sandy you are very helpful to me today and you have a nice day!

Sandy: Thanks James it's a pleasure talking to you and you have a good day.

bye... bye...

5.If the patient plan is PPO or POS now what will you do?

6.Sandy: Non covered as per Patient plan and the patient plan does not cover OON benefits

James: What plan does the patient have? Sandy!

Sandy: Let me find that James?

James: Okay

Sandy: James the patient plan is PPO

James: Sandy as per the Patient plan type that covers out of network so could you please send this back for reprocess

Sandy: James yes you are right, let's make a note of it and send it back for reprocessing

James: Thanks Sandy

Sandy: You are welcome James! ....and I sent it back for reprocess so please be allow 15 business days for review.

James: Thanks Sandy what is the claim?

Sandy: The claim is 884455

James: Is there any reference # for this call?

Sandy: Yes, James it is 0285

James: Thank you so much Sandy you are very helpful to me today and you have a nice day!

Sandy: Thanks James it's a pleasure talking to you and you have a good day.

bye... bye...

7. Non-covered as per provider contract, what will you do?

8.Sandy: Claim was denied for non-covered service.

James: Non-covered as per patient plan or provider contract?

Sandy: Non-covered as per the provider contract

James: What is non-covered in the provider contract?

Sandy: Provider is not eligible to bill this service

James: Okay Sandy, could you please hold for a moment I will check some additional information on this code?

Sandy: Okay

9.Now upon checking the patient history and found the same CPT code under this provider has been paid on different DOS what will you do?

10.James: Sandy thanks for been on hold, I really appreciate your patience, upon checking the billing summary of this patient we have received payment for this code under this same provider on different DOS, could you please verify that

Sandy: yes, please provide me that DOS

James: It is 10-30-2020

Sandy: Let me check this DOS James, so pls be on hold

James: Okay sandy

Sandy: Sandy at that time on dos 10-30-2020 provider have the same contract but it got paid so let me send this claim back for reprocess

James: Thanks, sandy

Sandy: You are welcome, I sent it back for reprocess so please be allow 15 business days for review.

James: Thank you so much Sandy you are very helpful to me today and you have a nice day!

Sandy: Thanks James it's a pleasure talking to you and you have a good day.

bye... bye...

11.Non covered as per provider contract but Found a payment on previous DOS but the rep refused to send for reprocessing what will you do?

12.James: Sandy thanks for been on hold, I really appreciate your patience, upon checking the billing summary of this patient we have received payment for this code under this same provider on different DOS, could you please verify that

Sandy: Sorry James we cannot compare claims so I cannot send back for reprocessing

James: Okay sandy can we send an appeal?

Sandy: yes you can!

James: The appeal address is PO BOX 740805 Atlanta GA 30374

James: What is the timely filing limit for appeal?

Sandy the TFL is 120 days from the date of denial

James: Thanks Sandy what is the claim?

Sandy: The claim is 884455

James: Is there any reference # for this call?

Sandy: Yes James it is 0285

James: Thank you so much Sandy you are very helpful to me today and you have a nice day!

Sandy: Thanks James its a pleasure talking to you and you have a good day. bye.. bye..

13.*now upon checking the patient history and found the same CPT code under this provider has been NEVER paid on any DOS what will you do?..*****

James: Sandy may I get the appeal address for my documentation?

Sandy: Yes the appeal address is PO BOX 740805 Atlanta GA 30374

James: What is the timely filing limit for appeal?

Sandy the TFL is 120 days from the date of denial

James: Thanks Sandy what is the claim?

Sandy: The claim is 884455

James: Is there any reference # for this call?

Sandy: Yes James it is 0285

James: Thank you so much Sandy you are very helpful to me today and you have a nice day!

Sandy: Thanks James its a pleasure talking to you and you have a good day.

bye.. Bye...

MOCK-AUTHORIZATION DENIAL:

1.Sandy: Thanks for calling this is Sandy, how may I help you?

James: Hi, my name is James, I am calling for Doctor's office and I would like to check the claim status for a patient

Sandy: Which Doctor's office you calling for?

James: I am calling for General Orthopedic associates

Sandy: What is your telephone number?

James: My telephone# is 800-999-9999

Sandy: What is the patient's SSN (social security number)?

James: The SSN is 123-456-789

Sandy: Could you please hold for a moment so that I can pull the patient records?

James: Yes, please!

Sandy: What is the patient's name and DOB?

2.James: The patient name is Linda Far and DOB is 11-26-1995

Sandy: What is the DOS you checking for?

James: The DOS is 07-26-2020

Sandy: What is the billed amount on this claim?

James: The billed amount is $1500.00

Sandy: Could you please hold for a moment so that I can pull up the claim?

James: Yes Of course!

Sandy: Thanks for being on hold James the claim was denied?

James: Okay may I know the claim received date?

Sandy: The claim was received on 08-15-2020

3.James: And what is the denial date?

Sandy: The denial date is 08-22-2020

James: May I know the reason for the denial?

Sandy: Claim was denied for no authorization on file!

James: Could you please hold for a moment; I will search for authorization?

Sandy: Okay!

James: Thank you so much for holding I really appreciate your patience! "Sandy I upon checking I cannot find any auth# in my system, can you please check whether any hospital claim was received on this DOS?

Sandy: Let me find that James?

James: Okay

Sandy: James I cannot find any hospital claim on this DOS

4.James: Can we get a retro authorization in this case?

Sandy: Sorry James retro auth is not possible!

James: Okay Sandy can we send an appeal?

Sandy: Yes you can!

James: What is the appeal address?

Sandy: Yes the appeal address is PO BOX 30432 SALT LAKE CITY UT 84130-0432!

James: What is the timely filing limit for appeal?

Sandy: The TFL for appeal is 365 days from the date of denial!

James: Okay what is the claim#?

Sandy: The claim# is 98745

James: And what is the call reference#?

Sandy: The call ref# is 8578.

James: Thank you so much Sandy you are very helpful to me today and you have a nice day!

Sandy: Thanks James its a pleasure talking to you and you have a good day. bye.. bye...

5.If the Place of service (POS) used is 23 in auth denial what will you do?

6.James: Thank you so much for holding I really appreciate your patience! "Sandy upon checking I found the POS we have used is "23" which denotes this is an "emergency service" so this couldn't be denied as no auth on file, could you please check it?

Sandy: Let me check that James?

James: Okay

Sandy: James you are right, the POS you have used is 23 since this is an emergency service I am sending this claim back for reprocess and please be allow 45 business days for the review!

James: Thank you so much Sandy and what is the claim#?

Sandy: The claim# is 98745

James: And what is the call reference#?

Sandy: The call ref# is 8578.

James: Thank you so much Sandy you are very helpful to me today and you have a nice day!

Sandy: Thanks James its a pleasure talking to you and you have a good day.

bye.. bye...

7.If auth# found in your system now what will you do?

8.James: Thank you so much for holding I really appreciate your patience! "Sandy upon checking I found auth# in my system, can I verify that with you?

Sandy: Yes James go ahead?

James: Thank you and the Auth# is A8765432

Sandy: James can I put you on hold to verify it?

 James: Sandy take your own time!

Sandy: Thank you, James!....James thanks for being on hold I verified and found the Auth# you have given is valid for this Dos.

James: Sandy can you please send this claim back for reprocess with this auth#

Sandy: Okay let me take a note on it and send this claim back for reprocess!

 James: Thank you!

Sandy: Thank you, James! I have sent it   back for reprocess and please allow 45 business days for review

James: Thank you so much Sandy and what is the claim#?

Sandy: The claim# is 98745

James: And what is the call reference#?

Sandy: The call ref# is 8578.

James: Thank you so much Sandy you are very helpful to me today and you have a nice day!

Sandy: Thanks James its a pleasure talking to you and you have a good day.

bye.. bye...

9.If Retro auth# is possible now what will you do?

10.James: Can we get a retro authorization in this case?

Sandy: Yes James retro auth is possible!

James: Okay Sandy how could we get the Retro authorization?

Sandy: Yes you can call the authorization department at 187-845-7892!

James: Okay what is the claim#?

Sandy: The claim# is 98745

James: And what is the call reference#?

Sandy: The call ref# is 8578.

James: Thank you so much Sandy you are very helpful to me today and you have a nice day!

Sandy: Thanks James its a pleasure talking to you and you have a good day.

bye.. bye...

11.If you found PAYMENT for the same CPT code without authorization# in previous DOS now what will you do?

12.James: Thank you so much for holding I really appreciate your patience! "Sandy upon checking I found the same CPT code was paid previously without any authorization# can you please verify that?

Sandy: Yes James what is that previous DOS?

James: The previous DOS is 01-22-2019

Sandy: James can I put you on hold to verify it?

 James: Sandy take your own time!

Sandy: Thank you, James!....James thanks for being on hold I verified and found this CPT code was paid previously without any Auth#.

 James: Sandy can you please send this claim back for reprocess with reference to the paid claim?

Sandy: Okay let me take a note on it and send this claim back for reprocess!

James: Thank you!

Sandy: Thank you, James! I have sent it back for reprocess and please allow 45 business days for review

James: Thank you so much Sandy and what is the claim#?

Sandy: The claim# is 98745

James: And what is the call reference#?

Sandy: The call ref# is 8578.

James: Thank you so much Sandy you are very helpful to me today and you have a nice day!

Sandy: Thanks James its a pleasure talking to you and you have a good day.

bye.. bye...

13.If the rep said HOSPITAL Claim was received on this DOS now what will you do?

14.James: Thank you so much for holding I really appreciate your patience! "Sandy I upon checking I cannot find any auth# in my system, can you please check whether any hospital claim was received on this DOS?

Sandy: Let me find that James?

James: Okay

Sandy: James I have found one hospital claim on this DOS

James: Okay Sandy can you please check any authorization# in that hospital claim?

Sandy: James yes I have found one AUTH# IN HOSPITAL CLAIM

James: Could you please send this claim back for reprocess with that Auth#.

Sandy: James I can send but I am not guaranteed whether your claim will be payable or not!

James: That's not a problem, Sandy, you can send it!

Sandy: Okay let me take a note on it and send this claim back for reprocess!

James: Thank you!

Sandy: Thank you, James! I have sent it back for reprocess and please allow 45 business days for review

James: Thank you so much Sandy and what is the claim#?

Sandy: The claim# is 98745

James: And what is the call reference#?

Sandy: The call ref# is 8578.

James: Thank you so much Sandy you are very helpful to me today and you have a nice day!

Sandy: Thanks James its a pleasure talking to you and you have a good day. bye. Bye...

MOCK-Diagnosis CODE(dx) IS INCONSISTENT WITH PROCEDURE CODE(cpt):

1.Sandy: Thanks for calling this is Sandy, how may I help you?

James: Hi, my name is James, I am calling for Doctor's office and I would like to check the claim status for a patient

Sandy: Which Doctor's office you calling for?

James: I am calling for General Orthopedic associates

Sandy: What is your telephone number?

James: My telephone# is 800-999-9999

Sandy: What is the patient's SSN (social security number)?

James: The SSN is 123-456-789

Sandy: Could you please hold for a moment so that I can pull the patient records?

James: Yes, please!

Sandy: What is the patient's name and DOB?

2.James: The patient name is Linda Far and DOB is 11-26-1995

Sandy: What is the DOS you checking for?

James: The DOS is 01-26-2021

Sandy: What is the billed amount on this claim?

James: The billed amount is $150.00

Sandy: Could you please hold for a moment so that I can pull up the claim?

James: Yes Of course!

Sandy: Thanks for being on hold James the claim was denied?

James: Okay may I know the claim received date?

Sandy: The claim was received on 02-10-2021

3.James: And what is the denial date?

Sandy: The denial date is 02-22-2021

James: May I know the reason for the denial?

Sandy: Claim was denied for the DX code is incorrect for the CPT code.

James: Could you please provide me the Dx code?

Sandy: The diagnosis code is z94.0

James: Could you please hold for a moment; I will search this diagnosis code in my system?

Sandy: Okay!

4.If payment not found on this DX code in the patient's claim history/previous DOS, now what will you do?

5.James: Thank you so much for holding I really appreciate your patience! "Sandy, can we send a corrected claim with the appropriate dx code?

Sandy: Yes you can

James: What is the corrected claim address?

Sandy: Yes the corrected claim address is PO BOX 30432 SALT LAKE CITY UT 84130-0432.

James: What is the timely filing limit for a corrected claim?

Sandy: The TFL is 90 days from the date of denial!

James: Okay what is the claim#?

Sandy: The claim# is 98745

James: And what is the call reference#?

Sandy: The call ref# is 8578.

James: Thank you so much Sandy you are very helpful to me today and you have a nice day!

Sandy: Thanks James its a pleasure talking to you and you have a good day.

bye.. bye...

6.If payment found on this DX code in the patient's claim history/previous DOS, now what will you do?

James: Thank you so much for holding I really appreciate your patience! "Sandy, upon checking the claim history I found this same Dx and Cpt code combination have been paid already on previous DOS , could you please verify that?

Sandy: Yes can I get that DOS?
James: The previous DOS is 07-15-2020
Sandy: Please be on hold James
James: Okay!

Sandy: Thanks for begin on hold James, I found this CPT and dx combination have been paid already so I am sending this claim back for reprocess, and please be allow 45 business days for the review!

James: Thank you so much Sandy and what is the claim#?
Sandy: The claim# is 98745
James: And what is the call reference#?
Sandy: The call ref# is 8578.
James: Thank you so much Sandy you are very helpful to me today and you have a nice day!

Sandy: Thanks James its a pleasure talking to you and you have a good day.

bye.. bye...

MOCK-Missing/invalid referral:

1.Sandy: Thanks for calling this is Sandy, how may I help you?

James: Hi, my name is James, I am calling for Doctor's office and I would like to check the claim status for a patient

Sandy: Which Doctor's office you calling for?

James: I am calling for General Orthopaedic associates

Sandy: What is your telephone number?

James: My telephone# is 800-999-9999

Sandy: What is the patient's SSN (social security number)?

James: The SSN is 123-456-789

Sandy: Could you please hold for a moment so that I can pull the patient records?

James: Yes, please!

Sandy: What is the patient's name and DOB?

  2.James: The patient name is Linda Far and DOB is 11-26-1995

Sandy: What is the DOS you checking for?

James: The DOS is 04-02-2020

Sandy: What is the billed amount on this claim?

James: The billed amount is $1500.00

Sandy: Could you please hold for a moment so that I can pull up the claim?

James: Yes Of course!

Sandy: Thanks for being on hold James, the claim was denied?

James: Okay may I know the claim received date?

Sandy: The claim was received on 04-18-2020

3.James: And what is the denial date?

Sandy: The denial date is 04-22-2020

James: May I know the reason for the denial?

Sandy: Claim was denied for the referral is missing/absent.

James: May I know what plan does the patient has? (HMO,PPO, POS,EPO)

Sandy: The patient type is HMO

James: Could you please hold for a moment; I will search for the referral in my system?

Sandy: Okay!

James: Thank you so much for holding I really appreciate your patience! "Sandy, I have found a referral in my system could you please verify it?

4.If you have found a referral in your system, now what will you do?

5.James: Thank you so much for holding I appreciate your patience! "Sandy, I have found a referral in my system could you please verify it?

Sandy: James could you please provide me that?

James: Yes it is 1234567

Sandy: James please be on hold

James: Okay Sandy

Sandy: James thanks for being on hold, As I checked the referral you gave found it is valid and active

James: Could you please send this claim back for reprocessing with that referral?

Sandy: Okay I am sending this claim back for reprocess, so please hold for a moment!

James: Okay take your own time Sandy!

Sandy: James thanks for being on hold, I sent this claim back for reprocessing, and please be allow 45 business for review.

James: Thank you so much Sandy and what is the claim#?

Sandy: The claim# is UAS5823

James: And what is the call reference#?

Sandy: The call reference# is my name and today's date

James: Thank you so much Sandy you are very helpful to me today and you have a nice day!

Sandy: Thanks James its a pleasure talking to you and you have a good day.

bye.. bye...

6.If you cannot find the referral number in your system also patient plan is HMO or POS, now what will you do?

7.James: Thank you so much for holding I appreciate your patience! "Sandy, I cannot find any referral in my system so do you see any referral on file?

Sandy: No James

James: Sandy can you please check any hospital claim on file, If you found can you check any referral# in the hospital claim?

Sandy: James I checked and I cannot find any hospital claim on this DOS

James: That's okay Sandy, May I have the PCP name (Primary Care Physician) and his phone number?

Sandy: James the PCP name is Mark Taylor and his Phone# is 1800-586-9321

James: Thanks Sandy and what is the corrected claim mailing address and timely filing limit for the corrected claim?

Sandy: Yes it is PO BOX 74088 ATLANTA GA 30374 and TFL is 120 days from the denied date.

James: Thank you so much Sandy and what is the claim#?

Sandy: The claim# is UAS5823

James: And what is the call reference#?

Sandy: The call reference# is my name and today's date

James: Thank you so much Sandy you are very helpful to me today and you have a nice day!

Sandy: Thanks James its a pleasure talking to you and you have a good day.

bye.. bye...

8.If the referral number is absent also rep telling you that the patient plan is PPO or EPO, now what will you do?

9.Sandy:Claim was denied for the referral is missing/absent.

James: May I know what plan does the patient has? (HMO,PPO,POS,EPO)

Sandy: The patient type is PPO

James: Could you please send this claim back for reprocessing since the patient plan type is PPO which doesn't require a referral?

Sandy: Yes James you are right! let me send this back for reprocessing, please be on hold.

James: Okay!

Sandy: James thanks for being on hold, I sent this claim back for reprocessing, and please be allow 45 business for review.

James: Thank you so much Sandy and what is the claim#?

Sandy: The claim# is UAS5823

James: And what is the call reference#?

Sandy: The call reference# is my name and today's date

James: Thank you so much Sandy you are very helpful to me today and you have a nice day!

Sandy: Thanks James its a pleasure talking to you and you have a good day.

bye.. bye...

10.If the referral number is absent also rep cannot find any referral, and pt plan is HMO, now what will you do?

11. James: Thank you so much for holding I appreciate your patience! "Sandy, I cannot find any referral in my system so do you see any referral on file?

Sandy: No James

James: Sandy can you please check any hospital claim on file, If you found can you check any referral# in the hospital claim?

Sandy: James I checked and I cannot find any hospital claim on this DOS

James: That's okay Sandy, May I have the PCP name (Primary Care Physician) and his phone number?

Sandy: James the PCP name is Mark Taylor and his Phone# is 1800-586-9321

James: Thanks Sandy and what is the corrected claim mailing address and timely filing limit for the corrected claim?

Sandy: Yes, it is PO BOX 74088 ATLANTA GA 30374 and TFL is 120 days from the denied date.

James: Thank you so much Sandy and what is the claim#?

Sandy: The claim# is UAS5823

James: And what is the call reference#?

Sandy: The call reference# is my name and today's date

James: Thank you so much Sandy you are very helpful to me today and you have a nice day!

Sandy: Thanks James it's a pleasure talking to you and you have a good day.

bye. bye...

MOCK-Co-ordination of benefits update needed/additional information requested from patient:

1.Sandy: Thanks for calling this is Sandy, how may I help you?

James: Hi, my name is James, I am calling for Doctor's office and I would like to check the claim status for a patient

Sandy: Which Doctor's office you calling for?

James: I am calling for General Orthopedic associates

Sandy: What is your telephone number?

James: My telephone# is 800-999-9999

Sandy: What is the patient's SSN (social security number)?

James: The SSN is 123-456-789

Sandy: Could you please hold for a moment so that I can pull the patient records?

James: Yes, please!

Sandy: What is the patient's name and DOB?

2.James: The patient name is Linda Far and DOB is 11-26-1995

Sandy: What is the DOS you checking for?

James: The DOS is 04-02-2020

Sandy: What is the billed amount on this claim?

James: The billed amount is $1500.00

Sandy: Could you please hold for a moment so that I can pull up the claim?

James: Yes Of course!

Sandy: Thanks for being on hold James, the claim was denied?

James: Okay may I know the claim received date?

Sandy: The claim was received on 04-18-2020

3.James: And what is the denial date?

Sandy: The denial date is 04-22-2020

James: May I know the reason for the denial?

Sandy: Claim was denied for the additional information requested from the patient

James: May I know what information you have requested from the patient

Sandy: We need Coordination of benefits update from the patient

James: Okay Sandy did you sent any letter to patient regarding this?

Sandy: Let me check James

James: Okay

4.Sandy: James we have sent out letter to patient on 05-08-2020

James: Did you received any response from the patient for that letter?

Sandy: No response has been received so far!

James: May I know how many letters you have sent to member so far?

Sandy: So far 2 letters has been sent out and also no response for both letters

James: Okay Sandy can I get the second letter sent out date?

Sandy: Yes it is 06-08-2020

James: Thanks Sandy can you please send one more letter (3rd letter)

Sandy: Okay can you please hold so that I make a note to initiate to send 3rd letter?

James: Yeah take your own time!

Sandy: Thanks for being on hold James, the 3rd letter has been send out today and this is the final letter that we can send.

James: Thanks Sandy could you please tell me how the patient could update the COB?

Sandy: James patient can call the benefits department in-order to update the COB

James: So what is the benefits department phone number?

Sandy: Yes, it is 877-852-4230

5.James: Thanks Sandy, Is there any time frame for the patient to update it?

Sandy: There is no time frame, but make the patient update it as soon as possible

James: Sure Sandy, could you please tell me when did the patient last updated the cob?

Sandy: The COB was last updated on 02-08-2019

James: Okay Sandy can we bill the patient for this claim?

Sandy: Yes you can bill the patient

James: Could you please send me the eob through our fax#

Sandy: Okay what is your fax#

James: Yes it is 1877-333-4567 and you can put the attention as my name James

Sandy: Okay fax request has been initiated and it will receive within 24 hours

James: Thank you so much Sandy and what is the claim#?

Sandy: The claim# is XYZ5823

James: And what is the call reference#?

Sandy: The call reference# is my name and today's date

James: Thank you so much Sandy you are very helpful to me today and you have a nice day!

Sandy: Thanks James its a pleasure talking to you and you have a good day.

bye.. bye...

6.If the patient already responded to the letters sent by the payer, also the COB has been updated recently, now what will you do?

7.Sandy: We need Coordination of benefits update from the patient

James: Okay Sandy did you sent any letter to patient regarding this?

Sandy: Let me check James

James: Okay

Sandy: James we have sent out letter to patient on 05-08-2020

James: Did you received any response from the patient for that letter?

Sandy: Let me check James

James: Okay

Sandy: James we have received response from patient also the cob has been updated recently, so let me send this claim back for reprocess, could you please hold for a moment?

James: Okay Sandy take your own time

Sandy: James thanks for being on hold, I sent this claim back for reprocessing, and please be allow 45 business for review.

James: Thank you so much Sandy and what is the claim#?

Sandy: The claim# is XYZ5823

James: And what is the call reference#?

Sandy: The call reference# is my name and today's date

James: Thank you so much Sandy you are very helpful to me today and you have a nice day!

Sandy: Thanks James its a pleasure talking to you and you have a good day. bye.. bye...

8.You have checked the billing summary/claim history and you have found payment on another claim DOS nearby to this claim DOS, now what will you do?

9.James: Okay Sandy could you please hold for a moment I check more information on this claim

Sandy: Okay I will be waiting for 2 minutes

James: Okay, thanks for being on hold, I checked the billing summary and found a claim for the DOS 05-08-2020 has been paid can you please check how it was paid?

Sandy: let me check James

James: Okay

Sandy: James this claim has been paid also the cob never updated I don't know how it was paid

James: Yes Sandy but we have received payment so can you please send this claim to reprocess with reference to the paid one

Sandy: Okay can you please hold so that I make a note and send this claim for reprocessing

James: Yeah take your own time!

James: Okay Sandy take your own time

Sandy: James thanks for being on hold, I sent this claim back for reprocessing, and please be allow 45 business for review.

James: Thank you so much Sandy and what is the claim#?

Sandy: The claim# is XYZ5823

James: And what is the call reference#?

Sandy: The call reference# is my name and today's date

James: Thank you so much Sandy you are very helpful to me today and you have a nice day!

Sandy: Thanks James its a pleasure talking to you and you have a good day.
bye.. bye...

MOCK-Patient policy terminated | Expenses incurred after coverage terminated:

1.Sandy: Thanks for calling this is Sandy, how may I help you?

James: Hi, my name is James, I am calling for Doctor's office and I would like to check the claim status for a patient

Sandy: Which Doctor's office you calling for?

James: I am calling for General Orthopaedic associates

Sandy: What is your telephone number?

James: My telephone# is 800-999-9999

Sandy: What is the patient's SSN (social security number)?

James: The SSN is 123-456-789

Sandy: Could you please hold for a moment so that I can pull the patient records?

James: Yes, please!

Sandy: What is the patient's name and DOB?

2.James: The patient name is Linda Far and DOB is 11-26-1995

Sandy: What is the DOS you checking for?

James: The DOS is 04-02-2020

Sandy: What is the billed amount on this claim?

James: The billed amount is $1500.00

Sandy: Could you please hold for a moment so that I can pull up the claim?

James: Yes Of course!

Sandy: Thanks for being on hold James, the claim was denied?

James: Okay may I know the claim received date?

Sandy: The claim was received on 04-18-2020

3.James: And what is the denial date?

Sandy: The denial date is 04-22-2020

James: May I know the reason for the denial?

Sandy: Claim was denied for the patient is not active on the DOS

James: May I know the patient policy effective and termed date?

Sandy: Yes the policy has been effective from 02-22-2019 to 02-21-2020

James: Okay Sandy could you please check that this patient has any other active policy on this DOS?

Sandy: James patient doesn't have any other active policy

4.James: Okay Sandy can we bill the patient for this claim?

Sandy: Yes you can bill the patient

James: Could you please send me the eob through our fax#

Sandy: Okay what is your fax#

James: Yes it is 1877-333-4567 and you can put the attention as my name James

Sandy: Okay fax request has been initiated and it will receive within 24 hours

James: Thank you so much Sandy and what is the claim#?

Sandy: The claim# is XYN5823

James: And what is the call reference#?

Sandy: The call reference# is my name and today's date

James: Thank you so much Sandy you are very helpful to me today and you have a nice day!

Sandy: Thanks James it's a pleasure talking to you and you have a good day. bye. bye...

5.You have checked the billing summary/claim history and you have found payment on another claim DOS nearby to this claim DOS, now what will you do?

6.James: Okay Sandy could you please hold for a moment I check more information on this claim

Sandy: Okay I will be waiting for 2 minutes

James: Okay, thanks for being on hold, I checked the billing summary and found a claim for the DOS 04-15-2020 has been paid can you please check how it was paid?

Sandy: let me check James

James: Okay

Sandy: James this claim has been paid also the patient policy has been renewed recently on 04-01-2020 so let me send the denied claim back for reprocess and can you please hold so that I make a note and send this claim for reprocessing

James: Yeah take your own time!

James: Okay Sandy take your own time

Sandy: James thanks for being on hold, I sent this claim back for reprocessing, and please be allow 30 business for review.

James: Thank you so much Sandy and what is the claim#?

Sandy: The claim# is XYN5823

James: And what is the call reference#?

Sandy: The call reference# is my name and today's date

James: Thank you so much Sandy you are very helpful to me today and you have a nice day!

Sandy: Thanks James its a pleasure talking to you and you have a good day.

bye.. bye...

7. If the rep said there is another new active policy under the same provider, now what will you do?

8.James: Okay Sandy could you please check that this patient has any other active policy on this DOS?

Sandy: Let me check James

James: Okay Sandy take your own time

Sandy: James thanks for being on hold, I found patient has a new active policy on this DOS

James: Okay Sandy can you please provide me the new policy number?

Sandy: Yes James the new policy# is 12345678

James: May I know the new policy effective and termed date?

Sandy: Yes the policy has been effective from 02-21-2020 and there is no termed date

James: So can you please send this claim to reprocess under this new policy?

Sandy: James I cannot send it back, since this is a new policy so the provider has to resubmit it

James: Okay and what is the mailing address and timely filing limit to resubmit the claim under the new policy?

Sandy: Of course, it is PO BOX 80669 SALT LAKE CITY UT 84230 and time frame is 365 days from DOS

James: Thank you so much Sandy and what is the claim#?

Sandy: The claim# is XYN5823

James: And what is the call reference#?

Sandy: The call reference# is my name and today's date

James: Thank you so much Sandy you are very helpful to me today and you have a nice day!

Sandy: Thanks James its a pleasure talking to you and you have a good day.

bye.. bye...

9.If the rep said there is a different payer is active, now what will you do?

10.James: Okay Sandy could you please check that this patient has any other active policy on this DOS?

Sandy: James patient doesn't have any other active policy

James: Could you please check that this patient has any other insurance active on this DOS?

Sandy: James patient has other insurance active on this DOS

James: Okay Sandy could you provide me that payer details like payer name, phone number, and policy#?

Sandy: Yes the payer name is BCBS of NY and I cannot find the policy number

James: Okay Sandy do you have the phone number to reach them?

Sandy: Let me check!
James: Okay

Sandy: James the phone number is 213-456-7896

James: Could you please send me the eob through our fax#

Sandy: Okay what is your fax#

James: Yes it is 1877-333-4567 and you can put the attention as my name James

Sandy: Okay fax request has been initiated and it will receive within 24 hours

James: Thank you so much Sandy and what is the claim#?

Sandy: The claim# is XYN5823

James: And what is the call reference#?

Sandy: The call reference# is my name and today's date

James: Thank you so much Sandy you are very helpful to me today and you have a nice day!

Sandy: Thanks James its a pleasure talking to you and you have a good day. bye.. Bye…

MOCK-DUPLICATE:

1.Sandy: Thanks for calling this is Sandy, how may I help you?

James: Hi, my name is James, I am calling for Doctor's office and I would like to check the claim status for a patient

Sandy: Which Doctor's office you calling for?

James: I am calling for General Orthopaedic associates

Sandy: What is your telephone number?

James: My telephone# is 800-999-9999

Sandy: What is the patient's SSN (social security number)?

James: The SSN is 123-456-789

Sandy: Could you please hold for a moment so that I can pull the patient records?

James: Yes, please!

Sandy: What is the patient's name and DOB?

2.James: The patient name is Linda Far and DOB is 11-26-1995

Sandy: What is the DOS you checking for?

James: The DOS is 04-02-2020

Sandy: What is the billed amount on this claim?

James: The billed amount is $1500.00

Sandy: Could you please hold for a moment so that I can pull up the claim?

James: Yes Of course!

3. You checked your system and found the claim was mistakenly submitted twice with the same information, now what will you do?

4.Sandy: Thanks for being on hold James, the claim was denied?

James: Okay may I know the claim received date?

Sandy: The claim was received on 04-10-2020

James: And what is the denial date?

Sandy: The denial date is 04-20-2020

James: May I know the reason for the denial?

Sandy: Claim was denied as Duplicate

James: Could you please check this claim was received as corrected claim or new claim?

Sandy: The claim was received as a new claim without any corrections

James: May I know the original claim status?

Sandy: The original claim was paid

James: What is the original claim received date?

Sandy: James the original claim was received on 04-07-2020

James: What is the original claim paid date?

5.Sandy: The original claim was paid on 04-17-2020

James: May I get the paid formation?

Sandy: It was paid for 800.00 with patient responsibility Co-pay $30.00, paid thru paper check....... here I have cut down the paid scenario, please check the -paid mock call-

Please use complete paid (if original claim paid) or Denied (if original claim denied) scenario question for the original claim status and finish the call*.

James: Could you please send me the eob through our fax#

Sandy: Okay what is your fax#

James: Yes, it is 1877-333-4567 and you can put the attention as my name James

Sandy: Okay fax request has been initiated and it will receive within 24 hours

James: Thank you so much Sandy and what is the original claim# & duplicate claim#?

Sandy: The original claim# ABC1234 & duplicate claim# XYB5678?

James: And what is the call reference#?

Sandy: The call reference# is my name and today's date

James: Thank you so much Sandy you are very helpful to me today and you have a nice day!

Sandy: Thanks James its a pleasure talking to you and you have a good day.

bye.. bye...

---

6. You checked your system and found the claim was submitted twice with the different information (Either CPT code, Dx code, Modifier, rendering provider, Medical records), now what will you do?

7.Sandy: Claim was denied as Duplicate

James: Could you please check this claim was received as a corrected claim or a new claim?

Sandy: The claim was received as a new claim without any corrections

James: Could you please hold for a moment so that I can check both claims

Sandy: Okay I will be waiting for 2 minutes only

James: okay...Thanks for being on hold Sandy, upon checking I found The primary Diagnosis code we have used on the duplicate claim is different

Sandy: Could you please provide me that DX code?

James: Yes it is H60.31 (Difuse otitis external)

Sandy: let me check... Yes James the DX code on the duplicate claim is different from the Original claim, on the original claim it shows H60.13(Bilateral)

James: Yes Sandy could you please send this duplicate claim back for reprocess?

Sandy: Okay please be on hold, James!

James: Okay Sandy take your own time

Sandy: James thanks for being on hold, I sent this claim back for reprocessing, and please be allow 15 business for review.

James: Thank you so much Sandy and what is the denied claim#?

Sandy: The claim# XYB5678?

James: And what is the call reference#?

Sandy: The call reference# is my name and today's date

James: Thank you so much Sandy you are very helpful to me today and you have a nice day!

Sandy: Thanks James its a pleasure talking to you and you have a good day.

bye.. bye...

---

8. You checked your system and found the claim was submitted twice with different information (Either CPT code, Dx code, Modifier, rendering provider, Medical records), but the rep unable to send the duplicate claim for reprocessing now what will you do?

9.James: okay.... Thanks for being on hold Sandy, upon checking I found the primary Diagnosis code we have used on the duplicate claim is different

Sandy: Could you please provide me that DX code?

James: Yes it is H60.31 (Difuse otitis external)

Sandy: let me check... Yes James the DX code on the duplicate claim is different from the Original claim, on the original claim it shows H60.13(Bilateral)

James: Yes Sandy could you please send this duplicate claim back for reprocess?

Sandy: Okay please be on hold, James!

James: Okay Sandy take your own time

Sandy: James thanks for being on hold, I tried to send this claim back for reprocessing but unfortunately, I am unable to send it since another claim was already paid on this DOS for this provider so the adjudication system cannot accept it now

James: That's okay Sandy what can we do now?

Sandy: James my suggestion is you can send an appeal to show that this not a duplicate claim

James: Okay what is the appeal address and TFL?

Sandy: Of course it is PO BOX 80669 SALT LAKE CITY UT 84230 and the time frame is 365 days from the date of denial

James: Thank you so much Sandy and what is the original claim# & duplicate claim#?

Sandy: The original claim# ABC1234 & duplicate claim# XYB5678?

James: And what is the call reference#?

Sandy: The call reference# is my name and today's date

James: Thank you so much Sandy you are very helpful to me today and you have a nice day!

Sandy: Thanks James it's a pleasure talking to you and you have a good day. bye.. Bye…

MOCK-INCLUSIVE | GLOBAL | BUNDLED:

1.Sandy: Thanks for calling this is Sandy, how may I help you?

James: Hi, my name is James, I am calling for Doctor's office and I would like to check the claim status for a patient

Sandy: Which Doctor's office you calling for?

James: I am calling for General Orthopaedic associates

Sandy: What is your telephone number?

James: My telephone# is 800-999-9999

Sandy: What is the patient's SSN (social security number)?

James: The SSN is 123-456-789

Sandy: Could you please hold for a moment so that I can pull the patient records?

James: Yes, please!

Sandy: What is the patient's name and DOB?

2.James: The patient name is Linda Far and DOB is 11-26-1995

Sandy: What is the DOS you checking for?

James: The DOS is 04-10-2020

Sandy: What is the billed amount on this claim?

James: The billed amount is $1500.00

Sandy: Could you please hold for a moment so that I can pull up the claim?

James: Yes Of course!

Sandy: Thanks for being on hold James, the claim was denied?

James: Okay may I know the claim received date?

Sandy: The claim was received on 04-18-2020

3.James: And what is the denial date?

Sandy: The denial date is 04-22-2020

James: May I know the reason for the denial?

Sandy: Claim was denied as CPT 97140 inclusive to another code on same claim

James: May I know to which CPT code it was included with?

Sandy: Yes CPT 97140 was included with CPT 97530

James: Okay Sandy can we send a corrected claim with appropriate modifier?

Sandy: Yes you can!

James: What is the corrected claim mailing address and TFL?

Sandy: Of course, it is PO BOX 80669 SALT LAKE CITY UT 84230 and the time frame is 120 days from the date of denial

James: Thanks Sandy and what is the claim#?

Sandy: The claim# is P458

James: And what is the call reference#?

Sandy: The call reference# is my name and today's date

James: Thank you so much Sandy you are very helpful to me today and you have a nice day!

Sandy: Thanks James its a pleasure talking to you and you have a good day.

bye.. bye...

4.You have checked the billing summary/claim history and you have found payment for the same CPT code on another DOS, now what will you do?

5.Sandy: Yes CPT 97140 was included with CPT 97530

James: Okay Sandy could you please hold for a moment to check for more information on this CPT code?

Sandy: Okay

James: Thanks for being on hold, I checked the billing summary and found CPT 97140 has been paid on another DOS can you please check how it was paid?

Sandy: Okay please provide me that DOS

James: It is 03-02-2020

Sandy: Okay let me check please be on hold James

James: Okay Sandy

Sandy: Thanks for being on hold James, I checked and found the CPT 97140 was previously paid so let me send this back for reprocessing.

James: Okay

Sandy: James I sent this claim back for reprocessing kindly allow 15 business days for review.

James: Thanks Sandy and what is the claim#?

Sandy: The claim# is P458

James: And what is the call reference#?

Sandy: The call reference# is my name and today's date

James: Thank you so much Sandy you are very helpful to me today and you have a nice day!

Sandy: Thanks James its a pleasure talking to you and you have a good day.

bye.. bye...

6.If the claim denied as globally bundled with another code, the DOS lies within the global period, now what will you do?

7.Sandy: Claim was denied as CPT 97140 bundled with another code

James: May I know to which CPT code it was bundled with?

Sandy: Yes CPT 97140 was bundled with CPT   97530

James: May I know it was bundled with the same claim or another claim?

Sandy: It was bundled with a different claim and that DOS is 04-02-2020

James: Okay Sandy what is the global period?

Sandy: Yes James the global period is 10 days

James: Okay Sandy can we send a corrected claim with the appropriate modifier?

Sandy: Yes you can

James: What is the corrected claim mailing address and TFL?

Sandy: Of course it is PO BOX 80669 SALT LAKE CITY UT 84230 and the time frame is 120 days from the date of denial

James: Thanks Sandy and what is the claim#?

Sandy: The claim# is P458

James: And what is the call reference#?

Sandy: The call reference# is my name and today's date

James: Thank you so much Sandy you are very helpful to me today and you have a nice day!

Sandy: Thanks James its a pleasure talking to you and you have a good day. bye.. bye...

8.If the claim denied as globally bundled with another code, the DOS lies after the global period, now what will you do?

9.Sandy: Claim was denied as CPT 97140 bundled with another code

James: May I know to which CPT code it was bundled with?

Sandy: Yes CPT 97140 was bundled with CPT   97530

James: May I know it was bundled with the same claim or another claim?

Sandy: It was bundled with a different claim and that DOS is 03-25-2020

James: Okay Sandy what is the global period?

Sandy: Yes James the global period is 10 days

James: Okay Sandy upon checking found the DOS is lies after the global period of 10 days, so can you please review it and send the claim back for reprocessing?

Sandy: Yes James you are right, please be on hold

James: Okay

Sandy: James thanks for begin on hold; I sent this claim back for reprocessing kindly allow 15 business days for review.

James: Thanks Sandy and what is the claim#?

Sandy: The claim# is P458

James: And what is the call reference#?

Sandy: The call reference# is my name and today's date

James: Thank you so much Sandy you are very helpful to me today and you have a nice day!

Sandy: Thanks James it's a pleasure talking to you and you have a good day. bye. Bye…

MOCK-PRE-EXISTING CONDITION:

1.Sandy: Thanks for calling this is Sandy, how may I help you?

James: Hi, my name is James, I am calling for Doctor's office and I would like to check the claim status for a patient

Sandy: Which Doctor's office you calling for?

James: I am calling for General Orthopaedics associates

Sandy: What is your telephone number?

James: My telephone# is 800-999-9999

Sandy: What is the patient's SSN (social security number)?

James: The SSN is 123-456-789

Sandy: Could you please hold for a moment so that I can pull the patient records?

James: Yes, please!

Sandy: What is the patient's name and DOB?

2.James: The patient name is Linda Far   and DOB is 11-26-1995

Sandy: What is the DOS you checking for?

James: The DOS is 04-10-2020

Sandy: What is the billed amount on this claim?

James: The billed amount is $1500.00

Sandy: Could you please hold for a moment so that I can pull up the claim?

James: Yes Of course!

Sandy: Thanks for being on hold James, the claim was denied

James: Okay may I know the claim received date?

Sandy: The claim was received on 04-18-2020

3.James: Okay may I know the claim denied date?

Sandy: The claim was denied on 04-22-2020

James: Okay may I know the reason for the denial?

Sandy: The claim was denied for pre-existing condition are not covered!

James: Okay is there any waiting period?

Sandy: Yes the waiting period is 15 days

James: Okay may I know the starting and end of the waiting period?

Sandy: Yes the waiting period is starts from 04-01-2020 to 04-15-2020

4.If the waiting period is active, now what will you do?

5.James: Can we bill the patient?

Sandy: Yes you can

James: Could you please send me the eob through our fax#

Sandy: Okay what is your fax#

James: Yes it is 1877-333-4567 and you can put the attention as my name James

Sandy: Okay fax request has been initiated and it will receive within 24 hours

James: Thank you so much Sandy and what is the claim#?

Sandy: The claim# P458

James: And what is the call reference#?

Sandy: The call reference# is my name and today's date

James: Thank you so much Sandy you are very helpful to me today and you have a nice day!

Sandy: Thanks James its a pleasure talking to you and you have a good day.

bye.. bye...

6.If the waiting period is over, now what will you do?

7.Sandy: Yes the waiting period is 15 days

James: Okay may I know the starting and end of the waiting period?

Sandy: Yes the waiting period starts from 03-20-2020 to 04-05-2020

James: Sandy the DOS lies after the waiting period can you please check and send this claim back for reprocess?

Sandy: Okay please be on hold, James!

James: Okay Sandy take your own time

Sandy: James thanks for being on hold, I sent this claim back for reprocessing, and please be allow 15 business for review.

James: Thank you so much Sandy and what is the claim#?

Sandy: Claim # P458

James: And what is the call reference#?

Sandy: The call reference# is my name and today's date

James: Thank you so much Sandy you are very helpful to me today and you have a nice day!

Sandy: Thanks James its a pleasure talking to you and you have a good day. bye. Bye.

MOCK-Claim PAID:

If the paid amount + patient responsibility is not equal to the allowed amount?

If Check was issued to the incorrect address?

rep accepted to reissue a new check

rep not accepted to reissue a new check

1.Sandy: Thanks for calling this is Sandy, how may I help you?

James: Hi, my name is James, I am calling for Doctor's office and I would like to check the claim status for a patient

Sandy: Which Doctor's office you calling for?

James: I am calling for General Orthopaedic associates

Sandy: What is your telephone number?

James: My telephone# is 800-999-9999

Sandy: What is the patient's SSN (social security number)?

James: The SSN is 123-456-789

Sandy: Could you please hold for a moment so that I can pull the patient records?

James: Yes, please!

Sandy: What is the patient's name and DOB?

2.James: The patient name is Linda Far and DOB is 11-26-1995

Sandy: What is the DOS you checking for?

James: The DOS is 07-10-2020

Sandy: What is the billed amount on this claim?

James: The billed amount is $150.00

Sandy: Could you please hold for a moment so that I can pull up the claim?

James: Yes Of course!

Sandy: Thanks for being on hold James, the claim was processed and paid already!

James: Okay may I know the claim received date?

Sandy: The claim was received on 07-25-2020

James: Okay may I know the claim Paid date?

3.Sandy: The claim was Paid on 08-05-2020

James: Okay may I know the allowed amount?

Sandy: The allowed amount is $100.00

James: Okay and what is the paid amount?

Sandy: Yes the paid amount is $75.00

James: Okay is there any patient responsibility?

Sandy: Yes the patient responsibility is $25.00 co-pay

James: Okay and the remaining $50.00 in the claim is for?

Sandy: The remaining portion is provider write-off/contractual adjustment

James: Okay thanks for this information Sandy

Sandy: You are welcome James!

4.James: Okay Sandy the claim was paid through Check or EFT?

Sandy: It was paid through a paper check

James: Okay may I know the check#?

Sandy: Yes the check# is 12345678

James: And the check is single or bulk?

Sandy: Yes it is a bulk check of about $1000.00

James: Okay and what is the check date?

Sandy: The check was issued on 08-06-2020

James: Okay could you please verify the check paid to which address?

Sandy: It was issued to the address PO BOX 54033 Belfast Newyork 78452

James: Okay do you have a cash date?

5.Sandy: It was cashed on 08-29-2020

James: Thanks, could you please provide the Eob through fax?

Sandy: Okay what is your fax#?

James: Yes it is 1877-333-4567 and you can put the attention as my name James

Sandy: Okay fax request has been initiated and it will receive within 24 hours

James: Thank you so much Sandy and what is the claim#?

Sandy: The claim# A12345678

James: And what is the call reference#?

Sandy: The call reference# is 56789

James: Thank you so much Sandy you are very helpful to me today and you have a nice day!

Sandy: Thanks James its a pleasure talking to you and you have a good day.

bye.. bye...

6.If the paid amount + patient responsibility is not equal to the allowed amount, now what will you do?

7.James: Okay may I know the allowed amount?

Sandy: The allowed amount is $100.00

James: Okay and what is the paid amount?

Sandy: Yes the paid amount is $75.00

James: Okay is there any patient responsibility?

Sandy: Yes the patient responsibility is $35.00 copay

James: Sandy upon adding the paid amount and patient responsibility is not equal to the claim allowed amount, could you please verify the payment information one more time?

Sandy: Yes James let me check!

James: Okay take your own time Sandy

Sandy: Thanks for being on hold James you are right the claim processed incorrectly

James: Okay Sandy could please send this claim back for reprocess?

8.Sandy: Yes James hold for a moment

James: Okay

Sandy: James I have sent this claim back for reprocess and a new payment will issue soon

James: Okay how long it will take Sandy

Sandy: Yes kindly allow 15 business days

James: Thank you so much Sandy and what is the claim#?

Sandy: Claim # A12345678

James: And what is the call reference#?

Sandy: The call reference# is 56789

James: Thank you so much Sandy you are very helpful to me today and you have a nice day!

Sandy: Thanks James its a pleasure talking to you and you have a good day.

bye.. bye...

9.If Check was issued to the incorrect address! The address not matching with the address in BOX 32 & 33! now, what will you do?

A. Rep accepted to reissue a new check

10.James: Okay could you please verify the check paid to which address?

Sandy: It was issued to the address PO BOX 1234 Belfast Newyork 78452(correct address is PO BOX 54033 Belfast Newyork 78452)

James: Sandy I verified our provider address and found you have issued the check to an incorrect address

Sandy: What is the correct address you have?

James: The address for our provider is PO BOX 54033 Belfast Newyork 78452

Sandy: Okay let me reissue the new check to the address you have provided, please hold for a moment

James: Okay take your own time Sandy

Sandy: James I have mentioned reissuing a new check to the correct address and a new payment will issue soon so kindly allow 15 business days

James: Thank you so much Sandy and what is the claim#?

Sandy: Claim# A12345678

James: And what is the call reference#?

Sandy: The call reference# is 56789

James: Thank you so much Sandy you are very helpful to me today and you have a nice day!

Sandy: Thanks James its a pleasure talking to you and you have a good day.

bye.. bye...

11.If Check was issued to the incorrect address! The address not matching with the address in BOX 32 & 33! now, what will you do?

B.Rep NOT accepted to reissue a new check

12.James: Okay could you please verify the check paid to which address?

Sandy: It was issued to the address PO BOX 1234 Belfast Newyork 78452(correct address is PO BOX 54033 Belfast Newyork 78452)

James: Sandy I verified our provider address and found you have issued the check to an incorrect address

Sandy: What is the correct address you have?

James: The address for our provider is PO BOX 54033 Belfast Newyork 78452

Sandy: Let me check

James: Okay take your own time Sandy

Sandy: James as per our record your provider updated with this address only and it was sent correctly

James: Sandy but as per our instruction and documents show the check should receive to the address, I verified with you so can you please reissue the check to the address PO BOX 54033 Belfast Newyork 78452

Sandy: James I cannot reissue the new check, if you still want to reissue the check to the new address please send the W9 form with the updated provider address

James: Okay how can we send the W9 form?

13.Sandy: You can send through Fax

James: So what is the Fax#?

Sandy: Yes the FAX# is 842-124-5890

James: Is there any attention to the fax?

Sandy: Yes you can put the attention to the Provider Credentialing department

James: Thank you so much Sandy and what is the claim#?

Sandy: Claim# A12345678

James: And what is the call reference#?

Sandy: The call reference# is 56789

James: Thank you so much Sandy you are very helpful to me today and you have a nice day!

Sandy: Thanks James its a pleasure talking to you and you have a good day. bye.. bye...

Terminologies in Alphabetic order:

1. Account Number/Encounter # - Number given by doctor or hospital for each and every patient's medical visit to track what is the i) medical condition, ii) treatment rendered, iii) Cost of the treatment rendered for that particular date of service. Block # 26.

2. Advance Beneficiary Notice (ABN) - A notice the hospital or doctor gives the patient before the treatment, telling the patient that Medicare will not pay for some treatment or services. The notice is given to the patient so that the patient may decide whether to have the treatment and how to pay for it.

3. Aging - One of the medical billing terms referring to the unpaid insurance claims or patient balances that are due past 30 days. Most medical billing software has the ability to generate a separate report for insurance aging and patient aging. These reports typically list balances by 30, 60, 90, and 120-day increments.

4. AMA - American Medical Association. The AMA is the largest association of doctors in the United States. They publish the Journal of American Medical Association which is the most widely circulated medical journal in the world. The AMA also publishes the U.S. for identifying physician and practice specialties.

5. Ambulatory Surgery (ASC) - Outpatient surgery or surgery that does not require an overnight hospital stay. Also known as "Day surgery" or "Same Day Surgery" or "Short Procedure Unit" or "SDS". Eg: Eye Laser Therapy

6. Allowed amount / considered amount/Approved amount - The dollar amount an insurance company deems fair for a specific service or procedure.

7. Appeal - A process by which patients or doctors/hospitals can object when they disagree with the health plan's decision not to pay for the billed services.

8. Appeal limit- The time frame that the insurance company gives to the provider to submit the claims & get reimbursed after the claim has been denied. The appeal limit starts from the date of denial. It is 120 days for Medicare & other insurance it varies.

9. Assignment of Benefits (AOB) - A written consent, signed by the policyholder/patient (in the absence of the policyholder) at the time of registration. This is to an insurance company, to pay benefits directly to the providers. Block # 13 in the HCFA 1500 form should have the phrase "SIGNATURE ON FILE". If not found, then the claim will be paid to the patient & not to the provider.

10. Authorization Number -The system whereby a provider must receive approval from a staff member of the health plan, such as the health plan Medical Director in the Dept UMR (Utilization Management Review) before a member can receive certain health care services. It relates not only to whether the service of the procedure is covered but also to

find out whether it is medically necessary. Also called as Certification Number/ Prior- Authorization Number / Pte-certification / Pte-admission approval. It'll be in the HCFA Block # 23.

11. Back Dating the Prior Auth- If auth is not used in that particular date & if the service is postponed, the request can be sent to insurance to use the same auth. If insurance accepts then it can be used. Need to explain why auth not used at the proper time.

12. Balance Billing- If the patient is enrolled with the secondary payer then the balance is billed to it. If the patient is not enrolled with the secondary payer then the balance is billed to the patient. This is called Balance billing. (Credit Balance)

13. Bankruptcy- Bankruptcy is a legal proceeding where an insolvent person can be relieved of financial obligations but loses control over bank accounts, and future financial options. Bankruptcy is a last resort for those with debt problems, and although while it may wipe the slate clean (to some extent) in terms of debt, it is extremely harmful to your credit rating, and will no doubt affect the way you are handled by financial organizations in the future. The patient can't be billed & look for the next insurance or else need to wait.(CB)

14. Beneficiary - Person covered by health insurance (enrollee or insured or subscriber or member) or who enjoys benefits may be "covered" or "dependants".

15. Beneficiary Eligibility Verification - A way for doctors and hospitals to get information about the patient's insurance coverage/benefits.

16. Billed amount of the claim/Charge amount of the claim- It is the Amount charged for each service performed by the provider. In other words, it is the total charge value of the claim. The billed amount for a specific procedure code is based on the provider. It may vary from place to place. It is not common across all the states.

17. Billing Office - The office which maintains the financial transactions of the provider. Eg: Access Healthcare, Omega Health Care, AGS Health, IHS, etc.

18. Birthday rule - The birthday rule is a rule in determining the primary and secondary insurance for a child when the parents are insured. It is calculated as per coverage of the parent whose birthday (month and day, not year) comes first in the year is considered to be your children's primary coverage.

19. Capitation- Fixed payments paid to a provider periodically for each patient assigned to the provider. The provider is

paid regardless of whether the patient is ever seen. The most common arrangement is Per Member Per Month (PMPM). In other words, a specified amount paid periodically to a health provider for a group of specified health services, regardless of quantity rendered.

20. Centers for Medicare and Medicaid Services (CMS) - A government agency that oversees the Medicare and Medicaid programs.

21. .CDM-Charge description master - Inbuilt software where all billed amounts for procedure codes are listed.

22. CDT (Current Dental Terminology) - Cpt codes for dental services.

23. Charity Care - Free medical care given to patients in financial difficulty who cannot afford to pay.

24. Claim - A medical bill/invoice sent to the insurance company.

25. Clean Claim - A claim is one that will pass through all front-end edits.

26. Clearinghouse - an entity that forwards claims to insurance payers electronically.

27. CLIA- Clinical Laboratory Improvement Amendments-10 digit. It'll be in block # 23 in HCFA 1500.

28. CMS 1500 - This is the form that doctors use to submit a claim to the insurance company. It has 33 blocks. Other names are HCFA 1500/CMS 1500/Provider claim/Medical claim/Professional Component/Provider Bills/ Medical bills/Professional claims.

29. COBRA Insurance - This is health insurance coverage available to an individual and their dependents after becoming unemployed - either voluntary or involuntary termination of employment for reasons other than gross misconduct. Because it does not typically receive company matching, It's typically more expensive than insurance the cost when employed but does benefit from the savings of being part of a group plan. Employers must extend COBRA coverage to employees dismissed for a. COBRA stands for Consolidated Omnibus Budget Reconciliation Act which was passed by Congress in 1986. COBRA coverage typically lasts up to 18 months after becoming unemployed and under certain conditions extends up to 36 months.

30. Coinsurance - A percentage the patient is responsible to pay for the cost of the medical services.

31. Collection Agency - A business that collects money for unpaid bills.

32. Contractual Adjustment (Discount) - The part of the bill that the doctor or hospital must write off (not charge patient) because of billing agreements with the patient's insurance company. This is only for contracted providers.

33. Coordination of Benefits (COB) - A way to decide which insurance company is responsible for payment if the patient has more than one insurance plan. This should be updated by the patient to the provider's office and also the insurances.

34. Co-pay - A small, fixed amount a patient directly pays a provider for specific services. It is an upfront payment a pt has to pay every time a pt visit a physician or Hosp. Also called "FLAT RATE" fee that is assigned as the out of pocket cost to see a par provider as each encounter.

35. Covered Expenses - Covered services are those medical procedures the insurer agrees to pay for. They are listed in the policy.

36. CPT (Current Procedural Terminology) - codes used to report services and procedures. These are level I codes under HCPCS.

37. CPT modifier - A two-character numeric descriptor used only with CPT codes.

38. Credentialing - The process used by health insurance companies to examine and verify the medical qualifications of health care providers who want to participate in the network.

39. Date of Service - The date (s) when the patient was treated.

40. Deductible - A fixed amount per contractual period that a pt pays before the health insurance will begin to pay; this is only paid if provider services are obtained. The patient has to meet the Deductibles every year. It is mostly patient responsibility and very rarely another payer pays this amount.

41. Demographics (Patient Demographics-PD) - Physical characteristics of a patient such as age, sex, address, etc. necessary for filing a claim. Also called as Demo sheet/Face sheet.

42. Diagnosis code - The illness of the patient- The conclusion reached about a patient's ailment by a thorough review of the patient's history, examination, and review of laboratory data.

43. Durable Medical Equipment (DME) - Medical equipment that can be used many times, or special equipment ordered by your doctor, usually for use at home. Eg: Wheelchair.

44. E Codes - Codes used to describe external causes of injury, poisoning, or other adverse reactions affecting the patient's health. This will be the secondary dx always.

45. Electronic Funds Transfer (EFT) - An electronic paperless means of transferring money. This allows funds to be transferred, credited, or debited to a bank account and eliminates the need for paper checks.

46. EMR(Electronic Medical Records)/EHR(Electronic Health Records) - This is a patient's medical record in digital/electronic format.

47. Emergency Care - Care is given for a medical emergency when the patient's health is in serious danger when every second counts. Pte-certification or Auth is not necessary for ER services. Block # 24 C marked as "Y" which is called an Emergency indicator. If not mentioned it will be denied by insurance even if the POS mentioned as ER/23.

48. Enrollee / Guarantor / Subscriber / Policyholder / Insured - A person who is the 'owner of the policy' or 'purchases the policy' or 'pays premium'.

49. E/M Services - Evaluation and Management (E/M) Current Procedural Terminology (CPT) codes are codes used by a physician to report services including but not limited to patient

history, examination, and/or medical decision making. These services are divided into broad categories such as office visits, hospital visits, and consultations.

50. Explanation of Benefits / Electronic Remittance advice/Remittance Advice (EOB/ERA/RA) - The notice sent to the patient and the doctor from the patient's insurance company after processing claims explaining the status.

51. Exclusions - Specific conditions or circumstances for which the policy will not provide benefits.

52. Federal Tax ID Number - A number assigned by the federal government to doctors and hospitals for tax purposes. Block # 25 in HCFA

53. Fee for Service - This is also called a Traditional or indemnity plan.

54. Fee schedule - A listing of the maximum fee that an insurer or health plan will pay for a service based on the CPT code.

55. Fraud and Abuse - Fraud: To purposely bill for services that were never given or to bill for a service that has a higher reimbursement than the service produced. Fraud includes offering and accepting kickbacks.

Abuse: The misuse of a person, substance, services such that harm is caused. Some of the healthcare abuses include excessive or unwarranted use of technology, pharmaceuticals, and services, abuse of authority, abuse of privacy, confidentiality, or duty to care.

56. Gate Keeper: Primary care physician (PCP) is also called a GateKeeper & also as a referring physician or referring doctor or referring provider. In HCFA, Name is in the block # 17, NPI # 17b, and Group #17a.

57. Global payment (Bundled Physician Rates) - Payment for provider & hosp are bundled i.e includes both the professional & the technical component if the same provider sends both the bills.

58. Global Days - All surgical services have been assigned a "global time period," lasting up to a maximum of 90 days, for post-operative care. All follow-up care for the surgery performed within the assigned global period will be considered part of the surgical reimbursement and not allowed separately. For major surgery, it is 90 days & for minor surgery, it is 10 days.

59. HCPCS - A coding system used to report procedures, services, supplies, medicine, and durable medical equipment.

60. HCPCS modifier - A two-character alphabetic or alphanumeric descriptor used with both CPT level I and level II national codes.

61. HIPAA(The privacy rule/act of 1996) - Health Insurance Portability and Accountability Act. This federal act sets standards and establishes requirements for disclosing what the HIPAA privacy law calls Protected Health Information (PHI). PHI is any information on a patient about the status of their health, treatment, or payments.

62. HMO (Health Maintenance Organization) - Must use the doctors and hospitals designated by the HMO. Need PCP & he'll be capitated under the insurance. Referral #/ referral letter is a must. OON benefits not covered.

63. Identify - To find or recognize.

64. Inpatient (IP) - A patient who has been admitted to a hospital and stays 24 hours or more. 65. Insurance company - An organization contracted with the patient to pay for his health care expenses. Also known as insurer or health plan.

66. Insured - One who has or is covered by an insurance policy.

67. Insured Group Name - Name of the group or insurance plan that insures the patient, usually an employer.

68. Insured Group Number - A number that your insurance company uses to identify the group under which the patient is insured.

69. Internal Control Number (ICN) / Document Control Number (DCN)/Claim Control Number - A number assigned to the bill/claim by the insurance company as soon as they receive a claim in their system. Medicare's claim # is called TCN (Transaction Control Number)

70. In Process - The claim is received by the insurance company and is being reviewed.

71. IPA - Independent Practice Association. An organization of physicians that are contracted with an HMO plan.

72. Itemized statement / 1-Bill - An itemized statement provides a complete listing or detailed account of every service posted to a patient account. It includes the DOS, description of services, service code, the charge amount, estimated insurance amounts, and totals.

73. Late charges - Charges discovered and processed after the initial final bill has been released.

74. Litigation - The period where the case is in court is called Litigation. Ex: No-fault insurance, Worker's compensation.

The patient can't be billed till the case gets over; other insurance can be billed if pt has. Need to wait for a response from the court.

75. Limited Policy - A policy that covers only specified accidents or sicknesses.

76. Limiting Charge - When a doctor does not accept assignment, there are limits on the amount he or she can charge you for most services. The doctor is allowed to charge 115 % of what Medicare approves. This is referred to as the limiting charge.

77. Lock-box - Lock-box is a banking term used when a hospital has a 'lock-box number at the bank for the checks to come in.

78. LMRP(Local Medical Review Policy) - LMRPs have been defined by CMS as "an administrative and educational tool to assist providers, physicians, and suppliers in submitting correct claims for payment" within a specified geographic area. However, the major goal of these local policies is to prevent the overutilization of clinical services paid by CMS. Their impact on providers and beneficiaries can be limiting coverage or denying claims outright. Now they are divided into 2, one is called LCD (Local Coverage Determination) & the other one is NCD (National Coverage Determination). URL is http://cms.gov/medicare-coverage-database/

79. Major Procedure - The global period for major procedures, as defined by Oxford, includes related Evaluation and Management (E/M) services provided by the physician on the day before, the day of, and 90 days after the major procedure.

80. Managed Care - Ways to manage costs, use, and quality of the health care system. All HMOs and PPOs, and many fee-for-service plans, have managed care.

81. Manual claims submission - The process of submitting health insurance claims via mail.

82. Medical Recording Index no (MRI) - It's maintained for 3 years in the sense after 3 years from the last visit to the doctor, then he is considered a New Patlent. The others are called Established Patient. After this, an account no. is given each visit is given a New A/C no.

83. Medical Record Number - The number assigned by your doctor or hospital that identifies your individual medical record.

84. Mother baby clause - Mother Baby clause is a rule in which a newborn baby is covered under the policy of the mother for a period of 30 days from the date of birth.

85. Medicare Automated Cross Over Claim - When claim information is automatically sent from Medicare the secondary insurance such as Medicaid.

86. Medicare Advantage Plan - (Part-C/Medicare HMO/Medicare Managed Care)

87. Medical Necessity - Medical information justifying that the service rendered or item provided is reasonable and appropriate for the diagnosis or treatment of a medical condition or illness.

88. Medically Necessary - Many insurance policies will pay only for treatment that is deemed "medically necessary" to restore a person's health. For instance, many health insurance policies will not cover routine physical exams or plastic surgery for cosmetic purposes.

89. Medicare Summary Notice (MSN) - The notice received by the patient and doctor from Medicare after processing of claims. It states, the amount billed to Medicare, Medicare's approved payment, the amount Medicare paid, and the amount to be paid by the patient. It also states denials if any. This is also called an Explanation of Medicare Benefits (EOMB)

90. Medigap - A Medigap policy is a health insurance policy sold by private ins companies to fill in the "GAPS" in

coverage under the original Medicare plan, like deductibles, co-ins & co-payments. Some Medigap policies also cover benefits that Medicare doesn't cover, like emergency health care while traveling outside the US. If pt has a Medicare Advantage plan, then this will not pay anything. They are Medicare's supplemental ins. Eg: AARP.

91. Minor Procedure - The global period for minor procedures includes related E/M services performed by the physician on the day of the procedure or during the specified postoperative period (periods other than 90 days) after the procedure (depending upon the complexity of the procedure).

92. Modifier - A modifier provides the means by which the reporting physician can indicate that a performed service or procedure performed has been altered by some specific circumstances, but not changed by definition or code assigned.

93. NDC (National Drug Code) - Drug products are identified and reported using a unique, three-segment number, identifies the Labeler, product, and trade package size. The NDC will be in one of the following configurations: 4-4-2,5-3-2, or 5-4-1. HCFA block # 23.

94. National Provider Identifier (NPI) - A 10-digit, intelligence-free, numeric identifier for providers and suppliers issued by CMS. HIPAA mandates the usage of NPI.

95. Network of Providers/Group Name - Under the same plan, a group of participating providers are there, they are called Network of Providers.

96. Non-Covered Charges - Service or procedure not listed as a covered benefit in the payer's master benefit list. These may or may not be billable to the patient.

97. Non-Participating Provider (Out Of Network provider/OON/Non-Par/Non-contracted providers) - A doctor, hospital, or other healthcare providers that are not part of an insurance plan's doctor or hospital network.

98. NCCI(National Correct coding Initiatives - The CMS developed the National Correct Coding Initiative (NCCI) to promote national correct coding methodologies and to control improper coding leading to inappropriate payment in Part B claims. The purpose of the NCCI edits is to prevent improper payment when incorrect code combinations are reported. The NCCI contains one table of edits for physicians/practitioners and one table of edits for outpatient hospital services. The Column One/Column Two Correct Coding Edits table and the Mutually Exclusive Edits table have been combined into one table and include code pairs that should not be reported together for a number of reasons explained in the Coding Policy Manual.

URL:http://www.cms.gov/Medicare/Coding/NationalCorrectCodInited/index.html?re direct=/NationalCorrectCodInited/ .

99. Observation - Type of service used by doctors and hospitals to decide whether the patient needs inpatient hospital care or can recover at home or in an outpatient area. It is usually charged by the hour.

100. OIG - Office of Inspector General - Part of Department of Health and Human Services. Establish compliance requirements to combat health care fraud and abuse. Have guidelines for billing services and individual and small group physician practices.

101. Onset Date - Starting Date of illness/treatment.

102. Out-of-Pocket Costs - The patient's share of the cost of health care services. This can include co-payments, co-insurance, or deductible.

103. Outpatient (OP) - Services performed at a facility where the patient stays less than 24 hours and is not admitted to the facility.

104. Over-the-counter Drug - Drugs not needing a prescription that you buy at a pharmacy or drug store.

105. Offset - When an insurance company makes a wrong/ excess payment to its providers, it would adjust the amount in its subsequent claims. This is called an offset. Refund is called Recoupment.

106. Ordering physician: He is a physician who orders non-physician services for the patient such as diagnostic laboratory tests, clinical lab tests, pharmaceutical services & durable medical equipment. Block # 17

107. Participating Provider (In-network provider/Par provider/Contracted providers) - A doctor or hospital who has contracted with the insurance company, has agreed to certain terms and payment conditions set by the insurance plan.

108. Payer id - It is an electronic mailing address to send claims electronically but not e-mail. It is 5 digits in the number. Ex: the path to find payer id list is https://access.emdeon.com/PayerLists/

109. PTAN (Provider Transaction Access Number) - It is given by Medicare to their par provider which is also called "Legacy provider identification number" or also "Medicare Pin".

110. Place of Service - This designates where the actual health services are being performed, whether it is home, hospital, office, and clinic.

111. Policy Number / Member identification number / HIC number (Medicare) - A number that the insurance company gives the policyholder to identify the contract.

112. Point-of-Service (POS) Plan - A plan offered by managed care. The primary care doctors usually make referrals to other providers in the plan. But in a POS plan, members can refer themselves outside the plan and still get some coverage.

113. PPO (Preferred Provider Organization) - A combination of traditional fee-for-service and an HMO. When you use the doctors and hospitals that are part of the PPO, you can have a larger part of your medical bills covered. You can use other doctors but at a higher cost.

114. Pre-Existing Condition - A health condition or a medical problem that the insured has before signing up to receive insurance coverage. Some health insurers may not pay for these health conditions.

115. Pre-registration - The function of this department can be categorized into three. They are i) Scheduling the patient's visit, ii) Collecting all the demo details, iii) Insurance Eligibility Verification.

116. Premium - Amount paid periodically by the Patient to keep the health insurance pian active.

117. Primary Insurance Company - The insurance company that is responsible for paying the claim first. If the patient has another insurance company, it is referred to as the Secondary Insurance Company.

118. Procedure code - The code used to describe the services/treatment provided by the doctor/hospital.

119. Provider - Any person (doctor, nurse, dentist) or institution (hospital or clinic) that provides medical care.

120. Provider Identification Number (PIN) - Assigned by the Insurance company/ health plan to their contracted providers. It is unique to each carrier & no specific format.   121. Rebill - To resubmit a claim.

122. Referral - A reimbursement requirement of some payers whereby a PCP must first refer a pt before the second provider's services will be covered. A patient needs to make sure that PCP issues a "referral" before she/he can visit a specialist or hospital. Box #23

123. Reprocess - If denial is incorrect & request insurance rep to process the claim over the phone is called Reprocessing.

124. Release of Information(ROI) - A signed statement from patients or guarantors that allows doctors and hospitals to release medical information so that insurance companies can pay claims.

125. Retro Authorization - Only in an emergency or certain contains the provider can get the retro authorization. Getting authorization after rendering the services within a prescribed time or day, then it is called retro-authorization no. The time period varies from insurance to insurance.

126. Secondary Insurance - The insurance plan that is billed after the primary has paid or denied payment.

127. Specialist - A doctor who specializes in treating certain parts of the body or specific medical conditions. For example, cardiologists only treat patients with heart problems. Also called as "Rendering provider" or SCP or "Attending physician" or "treating physician".

128. Self Pay or Private Pay - If a patient is not insured with a TPA or Payor then he must pay for all the services rendered to him in full. This is called Self Pay.

129. Stop-loss clause (or) Catastrophic Limit - The insurance company fixes the slab amount if the payee reaches the amount and the patient need not pay.

130 Superbill - A form listing procedure, service, and diagnosis codes used to record services performed for the patient and the patient's diagnosis for a given visit.

131. Supplemental - A supplemental plan usually picks up the patient's deductible and/or co-insurance, copay. This name is for Commercial & Medicare it is called Medigap.

132. Timely filing limit - The time frame that payers give to providers to submit the claims and get reimbursed. It is calculated from the date of service. For Medicare, it is 1 year & other insurance varies.

133. Third-Party Administrator (TPA) - An independent corporate entity or person (third party) who administers group benefits, claims, and administration for a self-insured company or group.

134. UB-92 / UB-04 (Uniform billing 92 / 04)/ CMS 1450/HCFA-1450 - A form used by hospitals to file insurance claims for medical services. It has blocks 81. Also known as Hospital claims/Technical Component/Institutional claims/Facility Claims/Hospital Bills.

135. UCR - Usual and customary Reasonable - The payment scale used in paying non-participating providers. Providers are paid according to the provider's usual fee, the customary fee

of other providers in the area, and the reasonable fee for the service.

136. Units of Service - Measures of medical services, such as the number of hospital days, pints of blood, kidney dialysis treatments, etc.

137. UPIN - Unique Physician Identification Number. 6 digit physician identification number created by CMS. Discontinued in 2007 and replaced by NPI number.

138. Utilization Review/Utilization Management/Case Management (UR\UM UMR) - Hospital staff who work with doctors to ensure an appropriate level of care for the patient's condition, arrange appointments with the primary and specialty physicians, obtain authorization #s, advise the patient of discharges, assist with the appeals process for denials received when applicable, etc.

139. V Codes - ICD-9 (diagnosis) codes assigned for preventive medicine services and for reasons other than disease or injuries.

140. Waiting Period - It is the length of the time given by the insurance company to the patient for a pre-existing condition. It may range from 6-18 months from the effective date of the policy.

141. Waiver of Liability - It is a document, signed by the patient, stating that, in case of insurance is not going to pay, or not covering the payment, the patient himself is liable for the payment. This is for commercial insurances.

142. Write off - Write off is the amount that is waived off by the provider. This is usually a loss borne by the provider due to various reasons.

143. W-9 Form - A tax form that certifies an individual's tax identification number. Helps to update the provider's contract, provider's mailing address & sometimes helps to verify credentials also. Some insurance will update all the details every year; need to produce W9 form that time. If no claim gets denied for the W9 form. (Comes under denial- pnd/dnd for addl info)

NOTES FORMAT:

1.NOTES Claim is SET TO PAY:

DOS   11/06/2020 as per review found the claim was submitted on 11/10/2020 and no response received yet, called payer UHC @ 877-842-3210 spoke with JULIE stated that the claim was received on 11/12/2020 and processed on

11/14/2020 and it is approved to pay, also rep confirmed that there is no denial on this claim. Rep said allowed $75.00 and set to pay $50.00 with pt resp Copay $25. Rep said the normal processing time is 30 business days from the received date so I verified the reason for the delay in processing rep said that there is no specific reason it is just due to backlog anyhow they will issue the payment soon, rep confirmed that payment will be out within a maximum of 15 business days from today. Therefore, please be allow some more days to receive the payment. Claim#12345 and Call reference# JULIE12212020. Thank you.

The claim is SET TO PAY, ACTION:
*   The claim was received and exceeded the normal processing time then ask the rep the reason for the delay in processing.

2.NOTES-PAID Claim Paid:

DOS 07/10/2020 as per review found the claim with billed $150.00 was submitted on 07/16/2020 and no response received yet, called payer UHC @ 877-842-3210 spoke with SANDY stated that the claim was received on 07/25/2020 and processed on 08/01/2020. The claim was paid on 08/05/2020. Allowed $100.00 and Paid $75.00 with patient responsibility Copay $25.00. The claim was paid through paper check# 12345678 under bulk $1000.00, check issued on 08/06/2020, and cashed on 08/29/2020. Verified the check paid to which address, the rep said it was issued to PO BOX 54032 Belfast Maine 78542. Requested the denied EOB through fax and it will receive within a day. Therefore, please wait for eob once eob is received through fax then send for posting. Claim# A213456. Call reference# SANDY12052020. Thank you.

Claim Paid, ACTION:

1. If the claim paid through a paper check and the paid date was more than 30 days then request the cash date.

2. If rep don't have cash date then request check trace

3. If the claim paid date was more than 30 days, then request the EOB through fax or mailing address.

3.NOTES-AUTHORIZATION Claim denied for NO AUTHORIZATION:

DOS 07/26/2020 as per review found the claim with billed $1500.00 was submitted on 07/30/2020 and no response received yet, Called payer UHC @ 877-842-3210 spoke with Sandy stated that the claim was received on 08/08/2020 and denied on 08/16/2020 stating no authorization on file. I checked the system unable to find the authorization# also verified the claim image no authorization was found in box#23, also checked the documents folder unable to find the authorization documents. So requested to rep to find any hospital claim was received on this DOS, rep checked and said no hospital claim found on this DOS. So verified the possibility of retro authorization rep said retro authorization is not possible. So requested the appeal information, rep said the appeal address is PO BOX 30432 SALT LAKE CITY UT 84130-0432 and appeal timely filing limit is 365 days from date of denial. I verified the billing summary no payment was found previously on this code. Therefore sending an appeal with medical records. Claim# 98745 and Call reference# 8578. Thank you.

AUTHORIZATION: Provider needs to get from the insurance

- It is the process of obtaining prior approval before providing a certain service to the patient. 2 types of authorization:

- a) Prior/Pre-authorization: Getting Approval BEFORE service

- b) Retro authorization: Getting Approval AFTER service.

4.NOTES-COB Claim denied for Co-ordination of benefits update/Additional information requested from the patient:

DOS 04/02/2020 as per review found the claim with billed $1500.00 was submitted on 04/10/2020 and no response received yet, called payer UHC @ 877-842-3210 spoke with SANDY stated that the claim was received on 04/20/2020 and denied on 04/25/2020 stating additional information requested from the patient. Verified what information needed from the patient, Rep said they need co-ordination of benefits update, so I verified any letter sent out to patient regarding COB update, rep checked and said the first letter sent out to patient on 05/08/2020 and second letter sent on 06/08/2020 and no response received so far. So, I requested to send 3rd letter rep accepted to send the last letter, also the rep advised me to inform the member to call their member's benefits department at 877-852-4230 to update it. Rep said there is no time frame but asked to update as soon as possible. Also, I requested the COB last updated date, the rep said it was last updated on 02/08/2019 at that time UHC is primary and no other insurance was found. Also, the rep said once the COB has been updated by the patient the claim will automatically get process, and the provider no need to call back to inform. Claim# XYZ5823 and Call reference# SANDY12/05/2020. Thank you.

COB, Action:

- check patient payment history if the payment on nearby DOS received from any other insurance as primary insurance then check the eligibility of that insurance and bill the claim to that insurance if the policy is active on DOS as primary.

5.NOTES- REFERRAL MISSING/ABSENT Claim denied for MISSING/ABSENT REFERRAL:

DOS 04/02/2020 as per review found the claim with billed $1500.00 was submitted on 04/10/2020 and no response received yet, called payer UHC @ 877-842-3210 spoke with Sandy stated that the claim was received on 04/20/2020 and denied on 04/25/2020 stating referral number is missing. Verified the patient plan type rep said the patient plan is HMO so referral is needed. Checked in system and claim form in box# 23 unable to find the referral number. Requested to check hospital claim, the rep checked and said hospital claim was not found. Therefore, requested the PCP (Primary care physician) name and phone number, rep said PCP name DONALD OBAMA & Phone# 800-586-9321. Rep provided corrected claim mailing address is PO BOX 74088 ATLANTA GA 30374 and timely filing limit is 120 days from date of denial. Therefore, please resubmit the corrected claim with referral#. Claim# UAS5823 and Call reference# SANDY09012020. Thank you.

REFERRAL, Action:

- Referral# is generated by PCP (referring provider) before sending the patient to the Specialist care provider.
- Patient plan HMO & POS it is necessary to visit the referring doctor, so referral# is required.

     Patient plan PPO & EPO plan does not require the patient to visit the referring physician, so referral is not required.

6.NOTES- Patient policy Inactive/terminated Claim denied for Patient policy terminated:

DOS 04/02/2020 as per review found the claim with billed $1500.00 was submitted on 04/10/2020 and no response received yet, called payer UHC @ 877-842-3210 spoke with SANDY stated that the claim was received on 04/20/2020 and denied on 04/25/2020 stating Patient policy not active on this DOS. Verified the Patient policy effective date and term date rep said the policy was effective from 02/22/2019 to 02/21/2020. Also checked in billing summary/claim history unable to find claim payment for other DOS after 02/21/2020. Also requested with the rep to find any other active policy on this DOS, rep checked and said no active policy found. Requested the denied EOB through fax and it will receive within a day. Also, I checked in system unbale to find other payer information. Therefore, need to call the patient for an active policy if the patient doesn't have any active policy, then the claim needs to bill the patient. Claim# XYN5823 and Call reference# SANDY09082020. Thank you.

Patient policy terminated, Action:

- The patient plan expires before DOS. or Begins after DOS.

- Call insurance and verify the policy effective date and term date

- Verify with rep any other active policy found

- If no other active policy found, then the Claim needs to bill the patient

Before billing the claim to the patient, check the web portal of the insurance if access is available to verify the patient eligibility information.

7.NOTES-DUPLICATE Claim denied for DUPLICATE:

DOS 04/02/2020 as per review found the claim with billed $1500.00 was submitted on 04/06/2020 and no response received yet, Called payer UHC @ 877-842-3210 spoke with SANDY stated that the claim was received on 04/10/2020 and denied on 04/20/2020 stating this is a duplicate claim. Asked the rep to find this claim was received as an original claim or corrected claim, rep checked and said it was received as an original claim so that it was denied as a duplicate. Verified the original claim status, rep said the original claim was Paid it was received on 04/07/2020 and paid on 04/17/2020. Paid $800.00 with patient responsibility Copay $30.00 paid through paper check for bulk check of $1000.00 under check# 12345678 issued on 04/25/2020. Verified the check pay to address found to be the same as PO BOX 54032 BELFAST MAINE 78452. Verified the check cash date rep said it was cashed on 05/15/2020. Requested both original and duplicate eob through fax back system and it will receive within a day. I checked the system found we billed the claim twice with the same information. Therefore sending the duplicate claim for adjustment. Original claim# ABC1234 and Duplicate claim# XYB5678. Call reference# SANDY09162020. Thank you.

DUPLICATE, Action:

- If two claims submitted to insurance with the same claim information.

- AR caller needs to call insurance and verify whether the claim received with the same information or not.

8.NOTES-INCLUSIVE Claim denied for INCLUSIVE | GLOBAL | BUNDLED DENIAL:

DOS 04/02/2020 as per review found the claim with billed $1500.00 was submitted on 04/10/2020 and no response received yet, called payer UHC @ 877-842-3210 spoke with Sandy stated that the claim was received on 04/20/2020 and denied on 04/25/2020 stating claim (CPT 78452) was bundled with another claim. Asked the rep to which CPT code it was bundled with; the rep said the CPT 78452 was bundled with CPT code 84321 on different DOS 04/01/2020. Verified global period rep said the global period is 10 days. The rep suggested before sending an appeal asked to send a corrected claim first with the appropriate modifier if the corrected claim is denied then send an appeal. Rep provided corrected claim mailing address is PO BOX 740805 ATLANTA GA 30374 and timely filing limit is 120 days from date of denial. I verified the billing summary no payment was found previously on this code. Therefore, sending this to the coding team to send a corrected claim with the appropriate modifier. Claim# P458 and Call reference# SANDY10102020. Thank you.

GLOBAL Action:

- If the DOS lies between the Global period range then it should be written off but there is a possibility to separate out the procedure with main surgery by adding modifier as well, so assign it to the coding team for clarification.

- What is Global Period?

- Certain post-operative services will not be paid for a duration of time stating that it was included in the previously paid surgery date of services. it is called global.

9.NOTES-PRE-EXIST Claim denied for PRE-EXISTING CONDITION:

DOS   04/10/2020 as per review found the claim with billed $1500.00 was submitted on 04/15/2020 and no response received yet, called payer UHC @ 877-842-3210 spoke with Sandy stated that the claim was received on 04/20/2020 and denied on 04/25/2020 stating a pre-existing condition are not covered. Verified about waiting period rep said the waiting period is 15 days, the start and end date of the waiting period is 04/01/2020 to 04/15/2020. Requested to send a letter to the patient, the rep said they have already sent a letter to the patient. Verified how many letters they have sent to the patient, the rep said they have sent all 3 letters, the last letter sent on 05/30/2020, so they unable to send another letter. Requested the denied EOB through fax and it will receive within a day. I verified the billing summary no payment was found on any dos lies between this period. Therefore, need to bill the patient. Claim# P458. Call reference# SANDY10152020. Thank you.

PRE-EXISTING CONDITION, Action:

- If DOS lies between start and end date of waiting period then bill the claim to patient.

- PRE-EXISTING CONDITION?

- If the patient having any illness or disease before taking the policy, those illness is called as pre-existing conditions that has to mentioned at that time of taking policy. If it is not mentioned claim will be denied as pre-existing condition.

10.NOTES-CPT & DX Inconsist Claim denied for CPT code is inconsistent Diagnosis code:

DOS 04/10/2020 as per review found the claim with billed $1500.00 was submitted on 04/15/2020 and no response received yet, called payer UHC @ 877-842-3210 spoke with Sandy stated that the claim was received on 04/20/2020 and denied on 04/25/2020 stating claim was denied for the CPT code is inconsistent with DX code. Verified about the diagnosis code rep given we have billed z94.0, also checked claim form found the same Dx code. Checked in billing summary no payment found previously with this CPT and Dx code combination. The rep suggested to send a corrected claim with the appropriate Dx code and the corrected claim mailing address is PO BOX 740805 ATLANTA GA 30374 and the timely filing limit is 120 days from the date of denial. Therefore sending this to the coding team to verify the CPT and Dx combination. Claim# 8324 and Call reference# 123. Thank you.

CPT & DX inconsistent, Action:

- If you found payment on any previous dos with this CPT & Dx code combination, give that DOS to rep to verify and ask to reprocess.

- If there is no payment found previously, then assign to the coding team to review and provide the correct Dx code, and once a response is received with the correct Dx code then send a corrected claim.

- Work as same for :

- CPT code is inconsistent with the patient's age, CPT code is inconsistent with the patient's gender (here CPT code needs to change).

- Diagnosis code is inconsistent with patient's gender, Diagnosis code is inconsistent with patient's age (here Dx code needs to change).

11.NOTES-Max Ben Claim denied for Maximum benefits have been met:

DOS 04/10/2020 as per review found the claim with billed $1500.00 was submitted on 04/15/2020 and no response received yet, called payer UHC @ 877-842-3210 spoke with Sandy stated that the claim was received on 04/20/2020 and denied on 04/25/2020 stating maximum benefits has been met. Verified about maximum benefits in terms of dollar or visit rep said max benefits reached in terms of visits. Asked rep how many visits rep said 12 visits allowed per calendar year and the max visits was met on DOS 01/03/2020. Requested the eob through fax and it will receive in 24 hours. Claim# 558. Call reference# SANDY10152020. Thank you.

Maximum benefits have been met, Action:

- If the max benefits were not met then ask the rep to reprocess.

- If there is a secondary payer then bill to secondary along with primary eob. If there is no secondary payer then bill the patient.

- Work as same for max benefits in terms of the dollar, how many dollars allowed, when was the last met.

12.NOTES-PRIMARY PAID MORE Claim processed as Primary Paid more than Secondary Allowed:

DOS 04/10/2020 as per review found the claim with billed $100.00 was submitted on 04/15/2020 and no response received yet, called payer UHC @ 877-842-3210 spoke with Sandy stated that the claim was received on 04/20/2020 and denied on 04/25/2020 stating primary paid more than secondary allowed. Verified the secondary allowed amount rep said secondary allowed $75.00 and also checked the primary eob found the primary already paid $70.00, so the $5.00 only secondary paid which was already posted in software and the outstanding $15.00 is provider write-off. Therefore, sending this to the posting team to adjust. Claim# WEC896 and Call reference# 4567. Thank you.

Primary Paid more than Secondary Allowed, ACTION:

- If the primary paid amount is more than the secondary allowed amount then write off/Adjust

- If the primary paid amount is less than secondary allowed then ask the rep to reprocess.

13.NOTES-NONCOVERED

Claim denied for NON COVERED SERVICE:

DOS 04/10/2020 as per review found the claim with billed $100.00 was submitted on 04/15/2020 and no response received yet, Called payer UHC @ 877-842-3210 spoke with Sandy stated that the claim was received on 04/20/2020 and denied on 04/25/2020 stating non covered under the patient plan, verified what is non-covered in the patient plan, the rep said the patient plan doesn't cover out of network benefits. Requested what plan does the patient has, the rep said the patient plan is Hmo. Checked billing summary no payment found previously on this patient account. Therefore, requested the eob through fax and it will receive in 24 hrs. Claim# 8979. Call reference# 55888. Thank you.

NON-COVERED SERVICE, as per patient plan (HMO)
ACTION:

- HMO and EPO plan doesn't cover OON therefore the denial is correct.

- PPO or POS cover OON then ask the rep to send the claim back for reprocessing

- If there is a secondary payer on DOS then bill the claim to secondary.

- If there is no secondary payer on DOS then bill the patient.

Notes for Non covered under provider contract:

- ......stating non-covered as per provider contract, verified what is non-covered in provider contract rep said the provider is not eligible to bill this service (CPT). Checked billing summary no payment found previously on this CPT code under our provider. Requested appeal address PO BOX 30559 ATLANTA GA 3074 and time frame is 90 days. Claim# 8979. Call reference# 55888. Thank you.

14.NOTES- MEDICALLY NOT NECESITY Claim denied for Medically not a necessity:

DOS 04/10/2020 as per review found the claim with billed $100.00 was submitted on 04/15/2020 and no response received yet, Called payer UHC @ 877-842-3210 spoke with Sandy stated that the claim was received on 04/20/2020 and denied on 04/25/2020 stating medically not a necessity. Checked billing summary no payment found previously on this diagnosis code and CPT code combination. Therefore, requested a corrected claim address PO BOX 31362 SALT LAKE CITY UT 30895 and the time frame is 120 days from the denial date. Also requested appeal address PO BOX 30559 ATLANTA GA 33589 and time frame is 90 days from denial date. Therefore, sending this to the coding team for review. Claim# 99966. Call reference# 89997. Thank you.

Medically not necessity, ACTION:

- Assign to the coding team to find correct Dx code, once response received from the coding team then send a corrected claim.

- If the coding team said the already billed Dx is valid no need to change then send an appeal with complete medical records to show this service was done as a medical necessity.

15.NOTES-TFL Claim denied for TIMELY FILING LIMIT (TFL) EXPIRED:

DOS 04/10/2020 as per review found the claim with billed $100.00 was submitted on 04/15/2020 and no response received yet, called payer UHC @ 877-842-3210 spoke with Sandy stated that the claim was denied on 06/25/2020 stating claim received after the timely filing limit. Rep said the claim was *received on 06/15/2020 and the normal TFL is 60 days from DOS. Rep asked to send an appeal with proof of timely (POTFL) also provided appeal address is PO BOX 30559 ATLANTA GA 33589 and time frame is 90 days from denial date. Therefore, need assistance to send an appeal with POTFL. Claim# 22255. Call reference# 6633. Thank you.

TIMELY FILING LIMIT (TFL) EXPIRED, ACTION:

- If claim billed within TFL then ask rep to reprocess.

- If claim filed after TFL, as mentioned in the notes please send an appeal with any POTFL.

- If claim was initially billed to different insurance within TFL, we can use that payer EOB as proof of timely.

16.NOTES-OFFSET Claim processed towards OFFSET:

DOS 04/10/2020 as per review found the claim with billed $100.00 was submitted on 04/15/2020 and no response received yet, called payer UHC @ 877-842-3210 spoke with Sandy stated that the claim was received 04/15/2020 processed on 04/25/2020 stating claim processed towards Offset. Requested the Allowed is $60.00 and the patient responsibility is copay $30.00. Requested to which patient account# it was Offset rep said the patient account is 666633, the Offset DOS is 11/02/2019 and the CPT code is 83214, also rep gave the overpaid check# 55777 issued on 11/20/20219 and cashed on 12/07/2019. Requested the eob through fax rep said it will receive within a day. Claim# 12213223. Call reference# 002. Thank you.

- Another possible reply from the rep stated due to HIPPA violence unable to disclose other patient details until or unless you verify that particular patient information So I cannot provide you the payment or patient details. In this case just ask the rep "what is that patient account#" document your notes as "rep refused to provide other patient payment details due to HIPPA violence but provided that patient account# is 1234567".

- OFFSET, ACTION:

- If the payer previously overpaid or paid incorrectly then the claim needs to send for posting to close the account.

- What is Offset?

- Sometimes payer might mistakenly have paid or overpaid to the provider also provider not responded/refund the overpaid amount to the payer then the payer will adjust that payment from future claims of that particular provider. Adjustment can be taken from any patient under that provider.

17.NOTES-POS INVALID Claim denied for Invalid place of service (POS):

DOS 04/10/2020 as per review found the claim with billed $100.00 was submitted on 04/15/2020 and no response received yet, Called payer UHC @ 877-842-3210 spoke with Sandy stated that the claim was received 04/15/2020 processed on 04/25/2020 stating invalid POS. Requested the rep to provider correct POS, rep doesn't have correct POS so asked the rep to check any hospital claim received on this DOS, the rep said one hospital claim received on this DOS and therefore requested the POS billed in that hospital claim rep said the POS in hospital claim is 21. Also, the corrected claim address is PO BOX 31362 SALT LAKE CITY UT 30895 and the time frame is 120 days from the denial date. Need assistance to change the POS, once changed corrected claim need to submit. Claim# 667799. Call reference# 88775. Thank you.

- Invalid place of service (POS): ACTION:

- If the rep provides the correct POS then update it and send the corrected claim.

- If the rep doesn't provide the correct POS then send it to the coding team to review and provide correct POS.

Important Interview questions:

1.Physical Address (OR) Facility: Denotes the Provider's office or facility is located. WHERE this entered in Cms 1500? BLOCK# 32.

2.Billing Address: Insurance company EOB and Cheques received to this address WHERE this entered in Cms 1500? BLOCK# 33.

3.Lock-box - Lock-box is a banking term used when a hospital has a 'lock-box' number at the bank for the checks to come in.

4.Clearinghouse: An entity that forwards claims to insurance payers electronically. Example: Availity, Office Ally, Emdeon, etc.,

5.Rejection: Claims will be returned from clearing office or insurance company is called rejection

6.Superbill/Charge Sheet? A form listing procedure, service, and diagnosis codes used to record services performed for the patient and the patient's diagnosis for a given visit.

7.Contractual Adjustment (Discount) - The part of the bill that the doctor or hospital must write off (not charge patient) because of billing agreements with the patient's insurance company. This is only for contracted providers.

8.HIPAA: Health Insurance Portability and Accountability Act to protect health records from third party.

9.PTAN: (Provider Transaction Number) It is the number given to all Medicare registered providers only.

10.Rules to submit CORRECTED CLAIM? After the claim details corrected, I will enter the word "CORRECTED CLAIM" in block# 19th and enter "7" in block 21 and I will submit it to the insurance company.

11.Mother baby clause - Mother Baby clause is a rule in which a newborn baby is covered under the policy of the mother for a period of 30 days from the date of birth.

12.Date of Birth Rule (DOB Rule):When mother and father is having insurance which insurance will act as primary and which will act as secondary?

As per the   birth-day rule, Mother 07/25/1994

 Here month will be considered not the year so as per above dob; mother's policy will act as primary and father's policy is secondary

13.Beneficiary (OR) Insured Person: A person eligible for receiving benefits under the insurance policy. He is also called an enrollee or insured or subscriber or member

14.W9 Form: Used for updating the provider billing office address and provider-related information with insurance.

15.Medicare Automated Cross Over Claim- When claim information is automatically sent from Medicare the secondary insurance such as Medicaid.

16.Explanation of Benefits / Electronic Remittance advice/Remittance Advice(EOB/ERA/RA) - The notice sent to the patient and the doctor from the patient's insurance company after processing claims explaining the status.

17.CPT (Current Procedural Terminology) - codes used to report services and procedures. These are level I codes under HCPCS. WHERE CPT code entered in CMS 1500? Block# 24D.

18.Advance Beneficiary Notice (ABN) - A notice the hospital or doctor gives the patient before the treatment, telling the patient that Medicare will not pay for some treatment or services. The notice is given to the patient so that the patient may decide whether to have the treatment and how to pay for it.

19. CLIA- Clinical Laboratory Improvement Amendments-10 digit. It'll be in block # 23 in HCFA 1500.

20. Coordination of Benefits (COB) - A way to decide which insurance company is responsible for payment if the patient has more than one insurance plan. This should be updated by the patient to the provider's office and also the insurances.

21. Co-pay - A small, fixed amount a patient directly pays a provider for specific services. It is an upfront payment a pt has to pay every time a pt visit a physician or Hosp.

22. Deductible - A fixed amount per contractual period that a pt pays before health insurance will begin to pay; this is only paid if provider services are obtained. The patient has to meet the Deductibles every year. It is mostly patient responsibility and very rarely another payer pays this amount.

23. Diagnosis code - The illness of the patient- The conclusion reached about a patient's ailment by thorough review of the patient's history, examination, and review of laboratory data.

24. E/M Services: Evaluation and Management (E/M) Current Procedural Terminology (CPT) codes are codes used by a physician to report services including but not limited to patient history, examination, and/or medical decision making. These

services are divided into broad categories such as office visits, hospital visits, and consultations.

25.Capitation -Fixed payments paid to a provider periodically for each patient assigned to the provider. The provider is paid regardless of whether the patient is ever seen. The most common arrangement is Per Member Per Month (PMPM). In other words, a specified amount paid periodically to a health provider for a group of specified health services, regardless of quantity rendered.

26.Point-of-Service (POS) Plan - A plan offered by managed care. The primary care doctors usually make referrals to other providers in the plan. But in a POS plan, members can refer themselves outside the plan and still get some coverage.

27.HMO (Health Maintenance Organization) - Must use the doctors and hospitals designated by the HMO. Need PCP & he'll be capitated under the insurance. Referral #/ referral letter is must. OON benefits not covered.

28.Point-of-Service (POS) Plan - A plan offered by managed care. The primary care doctors usually make referrals to other providers in the plan. But in a POS plan, members can refer themselves outside the plan and still get some coverage.

29.PPO (Preferred Provider Organization) - A combination of traditional fee-for-service and an HMO. When you use the doctors and hospitals that are part of the PPO, you can have a larger part of your medical bills covered. You can use other doctors but at a higher cost.

30.Pre-Existing Condition - A health condition or a medical problem that the insured has before signing up to receive insurance coverage. Some health insurers may not pay for these health conditions.

31.Referral - A reimbursement requirement of some payers whereby a PCP must first refer a pt before the second provider's services will be covered. A patient needs to make sure that PCP issues a "referral" before she/he can visit a specialist or hospital. Box #23

32.Release of Information (ROI) - A signed statement from patients or guarantors that allows doctors and hospitals to release medical information so that insurance companies can pay claims.

33.Authorization Number -The system whereby a provider must receive approval from the insurance if the provider does some high-dollar services. Health plan Medical Director in the Dept UMR (Utilization Management Review) before a member can receive certain health care services. It relates not only to whether the service of the procedure is covered but also to find out whether it is medically necessary. Also called as Certification Number/ Prior-Authorization Number / Pre-certification / Pte-admission approval. It'll be in the HCFA Block # 23.

34.Retro Authorization: Only in an emergency or certain contains the provider can get the retro authorization. Getting authorization after rendering the services within a prescribed time or day, then it is called retro-authorization no. The time period varies from insurance to insurance.

35.Specialist - A doctor who specializes in treating certain parts of the body or specific medical conditions. For example, cardiologists only treat patients with heart problems. Also called as "Rendering provider" or SCP or "Attending physician" or "treating physician".

36.Ordering physician: He is a physician who orders for non-physician services for the patient such as diagnostic laboratory tests, clinical lab tests, pharmaceutical services & durable medical equipment. Block # 17

37.Participating Provider (In-network provider/Par provider/Contracted providers) - A doctor or hospital who has contracted with the insurance company, has agreed to certain terms and payment conditions set by the insurance plan.

38.Non-Participating Provider (Out Of Network provider/OON/Non-Par/Non-contracted providers) - A doctor, hospital, or another healthcare provider that is not part of an insurance plan's doctor or hospital network.

39.HOSPICE: It provides Medical care and treatment for persons who will be dying soon. Hospice modifier

GV= When a physician is providing a service that is related to hospice (Physician is not associated with the hospice just attending physician.)

GW= When a physician is providing a service that is NOT related to hospice (Physician is not associated with the hospice just attending physician.)

40.GateKeeper: Primary care physician (PCP) is also called as GateKeeper & also as a referring physician or referring doctor or referring provider. In HCFA, Name is in the block # 17, NPI # 17b, and Group #17a.

41.Global payment (Bundled Physician Rates)- Payment for provider & hosp are bundled i.e includes both the professional & the technical component if the same provider sends both the bills.

42.Global Days - All surgical services have been assigned a "global time period," lasting up to a maximum of 90 days, for post-operative care. All follow-up care for the surgery performed within the assigned global period will be considered part of the surgical reimbursement and not allowed

43.Place of service (POS): (CMS1500 Block# 24B)

It is the place where service is rendered.

11- Office visit

21- Inpatient

22- Outpatient

23- Emergency

24- Ambulatory services

31- Skilled Nursing Facility

32- Nursing Facility

44.Modifier: (CMS1500 Block# 24D)

It gives additional meaning without changing its original meaning

24 = Unrelated E/M service by the same doctor during a post-operative period.

25 = (Very common) The medical provider did extra work on the spot.

26 = Technical component (TC). There is both a professional and technical component to this procedure.

27 = (Not as common) Patient has multiple visits on the same day, by the same or different physician.

51 = Multiple procedures by the same provider at the same session.

59 = Linked services by the medical provider.

76 = Repeated by the same medical provider on the same day, but separate sessions (excluding surgical codes).

GV= When a physician is providing a service that is related to hospice (Physician is not associated with the hospice just attending physician.)

GW= When a physician is providing a service that is NOT related to hospice (Physician is not associated with the hospice just attending physician.)

Tell me about yourself:

• Good morning Madam/Sir, thank you for giving me this opportunity to introduce myself •My name is Ajith and my native is Madurai • I graduated with a degree in computer application from Oxford college, Chennai. • In 2019, I was in the final year of college, During that time, I took the bold step of trying my hand at public speaking. I joined the debate club in my college. Preparing a presentation and talking about it in front of an audience, and then getting back to them with answers in the question and answer round motivates me! From there I have always believed that I should work in an industry that puts my speaking skills to good use. • Now coming to my family background, In my family there are 4 members including me. My father is a farmer and my mother is a homemaker. I have one elder brother he working in the marketing field. • My hobbies are watching movies, traveling and surfing the net. • •**My strength is I am a self-motivated, quick learner, and easy to mingle with team members. • My weakness is I am somewhat lazy but I am trying to do my work faster now. • My short-term goal is to get a challenging job where I can utilize my skills for the growth of the organization as well as to enhance myself. • My long-term goal is to achieve a good position where I can build my career and help the organization too. • That's all about me, thank you.**

All insurance phone number and website list please contact us:

FOLLOW US/Join in VBILLINGS FAMILY:

Website: https://vbcareer.com/

YouTube:

https://www.youtube.com/channel/UCtqFFg9hxpUn8xHarCqcgeg

Instagram: https://www.instagram.com/vbcareer/

LinkedIn: https://www.linkedin.com/in/vbcareer-vbillings-52838b209/

Facebook: https://www.facebook.com/Vbcareer-100379945475868

Telegram: https://t.me/vbillings

Email: vijaisun11@gmail.com

AR Training, AR Refreshing, JOB assistance & placement for both fresher and experienced

Contact V BILLINGS

Email: vijaisun11@gmail.com

Subscribe to our YouTube Channel:

V BILLINGS

9 798514 851584